ENDORSEM

"The Hybrid Leader is a remarkable understanding of what it will take to drive future business to succeed. The blending of the male and female strengths will create a brilliant, unified, collaborative effort. It is a concept for which the time has come. Any business which pays heed cannot help but succeed."

— Juanell Teague, Author of *The Zig Ziglar Difference: How the Greatest Motivational Speaker of the Century Has Changed Lives)*

"Trudy's work on the Hybrid Leader provides the formula for organizations to move from talking about people as their greatest asset to creating leaders who can bring the talk to life. Any executive who is serious about getting better results should read this book."

— Vicki Felker, Director, Nestle Purina Pet Care

"The book presents a unique perspective on male/female leadership issues. It allows people to remain who they are while seeing the addition of new strengths as growth, rather than surrender. A must read for anyone serious about leading in the 21st century".

— Isabel L. Kersen, PhD and Author of *POWER IS NOT A 4-LETTER WORD: How Women Can Claim Personal Power to Get More of What They Want in Their Lives*

"If Trudy does anything, she makes you think and rethink. And so does her book. You find yourself thinking about ways to improve yourself, your business and those you care for. A very thought-provoking read. I highly recommend it."

— Marty Scirratt, Managing Director of Sales Performance Improvement, Administaff

"I have such a better leader and person as a result of taking true ownership of defining my leadership principles. Refining my belief and commitment to collaboration has made all the difference in the world! Trudy's work around the hybrid leadership style is exactly what is needed to help leaders create environments where everyone feels like they can truly make a difference!"

— Maurice Morgane, Director of Sales, Chiquita

"There is personal and professional power in the principles that Trudy has developed in the hybrid leadership principles. I have watched Trudy refine her own leadership style to mirror the hybrid leadership style. Her committed to developing others is something that I have personally benefited from. Anyone who truly wants to be a leader, who can make a difference in the lives of others, should embrace these principles!"

— Virginia Morris, Director, Kahlua & Kuya, Allied Domecq Spirits and Wine, USA

"Trudy's work is cutting edge, insightful and right on target for America's workforce today. The work that she has done on hybrid leader is a clear demonstration of her commitment to build authentic leaders! This is exactly what the business world needs. Bravo!"

— Chris Thrash, President/CEO, Chris Thrash & Associates/Harvington Media, Inc.

"I had never thought about the concept of serving others as a core value of becoming a leader. I have always thought that the primary focus of a leader was to get results. As a result of gaining an in-depth appreciation for the principles and behaviors that drive the hybrid leadership style, I now understand that it's not just getting results but how those results are achieved. Adopting the hybrid leader concepts has given me the confidence to take the next step in my career as a value added leader."

— Jason Murray, Sales Representative, Wyeth Pharmaceuticals

"Trudy's beliefs and insights on leadership principles have had an enormous impact upon shaping my conviction to add more value and make a difference in the work place. I have personally tested the impact of building collaboration cross functional relationship (one of the core Hybrid Leader Principles) and can honestly say that the being vested in others success has been the key to achieving breakthrough results. Thank you Trudy for helping me to unlock the hybrid leader in me!"

—Tom Pellizzetti, Category Manager, Tyson Foods

"The hybrid leader concept gives us the language, which we have not had before, to speak about the importance of men and women finding ways to leverage each other's strengths. I want my children to work in a world where they can give value and be valued. The hybrid leadership concept is a step in the right direction to creating work environments where everyone can thrive."

— Barry Stevens, National Account Executive, Staples

"Gender differences can complement each other if we take the learning and apply them to our present cultures. Diversity among men and women and integration of all cultures is the key to working together more effectively and in making hybrid leaders necessary in all successful organizations. Trudy takes on a critical challenge in her work on the hybrid leader and offers hope to anyone who wants to improve as a leader."

— Sandee Nielander,co-author with Rob Poole, Ph..D. , of the
    forthcoming book, *Successful Transitions to Accelerated Relationships*

"My generation, generation Y is only going to want to work for a leader who displays the principles of a Hybrid Leader. Any company that wants to tap into the generations that hold the key to sustained success should embrace the Hybrid Leadership style. It's not optional. It's a must!

— Ashley Hansen, Director of Customer Relationship Management, CWE

THE HYBRID LEADER

THE HYBRID LEADER

Blending the Best of the Male and Female Leadership Styles

Trudy Bourgeois

OAKHILL PRESS
Winchester, VA

10 9 8 7 6 5 4 3 2 1

Printed in the United States of America
Cover design by Janice B. Benight
Text design and formatting by Bookwrights Design, www.bookwrights.com

Library of Congress Cataloging-in-Publication Data
Bourgeois, Trudy.
   The hybrid leader : blending the best of the male and female leadership styles / Trudy Bourgeois.
      p. cm.
Includes bibliographical references.
ISBN 1-886939-75-6
1. Leadership. I. Title.
HD57.7.B686 2005
658.4'092–dc22   2005016272

Oakhill Press
1647 Cedar Grove Road
Winchester, VA 22603
800-32-books

Contents

Acknowledgments   xiii
Introduction   xv

PART 1: THE PAIN

Chapter 1: Something Is Wrong with This Picture   3

Disconnected Employees   3
It Takes More Than a Paycheck   6
Give Me Credit for My Contributions, Would Ya, Please?   7
Right People, Right Bus, Wrong Driver   10

Chapter 2: The Impact of the Pain   13

The Cost of the Problem   13
All for One and One for One: Are We on the
    Same Team?   15
Silos, Turf Wars, and Infighting   17
The Negative Impact of Personal Agendas   19
The Business World Is Looking for a Few Good Leaders   21
Command-and-Control Leadership Wrapped in Egos   24
Let's Use the Entire Workforce, Why Don't We?   27

Chapter 3: How Did We Get Here?   33

Understanding the Changing Workforce   33
Diversity Redefined in Twenty-first-Century Language   42
I'm More Than Just an Employee   45

Employee Skills Not Being Optimized? Go Figure   47
Risk Takers Arise   49

PART 2: THE SOLUTION

Chapter 4: It's Time for a New Leadership Style   55

What Employees Need and Want in a Leader   55
A New Twist on Leadership: Introducing the
  Hybrid Leader   56
Hybrid Leader Anchors and Tenets   66
Leadership: Men and Women   67
Men and Women in the Workplace   69
Motivating the Team   76
The Root System of a Hybrid Leader   79
The Hybrid Leader Competency Matrix   81
The Blending Comes Alive   83
A Closer Look at Your Own Personal Belief System   84
A Hybrid Leader's Personal Business Principles   86
Ethical Behavior   86

Chapter 5: The Hybrid Leader at Work   89

Focusing on the Core   89
Do As I Do   91
Going with the Flow   91
Emotional Discipline   92
Strategic Planning   92
Extreme Communication   94
A Leader Worthy of Followers   94
Employees Are People, Too   96
Meet Them Where They Are   97
Business Development, the Hybrid Leader Way   99
True Service to Others   100
Eliciting the Greatest Contribution   101
Part of the Bigger Picture   102
Getting (and Keeping) Top Talent   103
Diversity Redefined for the Twenty-first Century   105

Breaking the Silos   106
Innovation   107
Advancing the Company's Vision   109

Chapter 6: Building Teams the Hybrid Leader Way   111

Working for a Common Goal   111
Step One: Collaborative Teams   112
Step Two: Collaborative Cross-Functional Teams   113
Step Three: Collaborative Cross-Functional
    Stretchpoint Teams   113
Quantum Performance Leaps: Creating Stretchpoint
    Teams   114
The Power of Common Vision   115
Real-Time Learning   116
Reinventing the Rules   118
Work Hard, Play Hard, Then Celebrate   121

PART 3: THE BENEFITS

**Chapter 7: The Benefits of the Hybrid Leadership
    Style: Case Studies**   125

Yes, You Really Can Make It Work   125

PART 4: MAKING THE TRANSFORMATION

Chapter 8: Applying the Knowledge   137

Put Yourself First (for the Moment)   139
Valuing People   143
Why Is Change So Difficult   145
Leadership Challenge: Team Performance Improvement   147
Leadership Challenge: Culture Change   148
Leadership Challenge: Black Women Perceived to
    Be "Angry Black Women"   149
Leadership Challenge: Innovation for Future Success   151
Leadership Challenge: Personal Growth   152
Leadership Challenge: Change   154

Leadership Challenge: Retaining Great Bench Strength 155
Leadership Challenge: Inclusion 157
Leadership Challenge: Conflict 158
Leadership Challenge: Ambiguity 159
Leadership Challenge: Women at the Top 160

Afterword 163

About the Author 165

Appendix A: Seven Key Hybrid Leadership Principles 167

Appendix B: Tips to Make the Transformation to
   Hybrid Leader 169

Appendix C: Suggested Resources 173

Appendix D: Personal Transformation Model 175

Selected Bibliography 177

Index 181

Recommended Reading 187

Developmental Resources for Success 189

Acknowledgments

As one of ten children growing up in the Deep South in a small three-bedroom, one-bath house, I could never have imagined reaching a point in life where I would have called that experience a blessing. I am now at that point. As I reflect upon my life's journey I am forever grateful to my parents, Clovis and Gerdiest Reid, who instilled the confidence in every one of their children that girls and boys were capable of doing the same things in life. I had no idea that the seed that was planted then would shape my purpose in life.

I am also grateful to my husband of twenty-five years, Mike, who was willing to choose a "nontraditional" woman as a partner. He has always been the supportive husband of a woman who aspired to reach the top before it became acceptable to do so.

To my now-grown children, Adam and MaryEllen, you will always be little ones in my heart. I hope that you both will have the courage to face the world with a commitment that embodies the principles and philosophies of the Hybrid Leader!

Introduction

I initially set out to gain a better understanding of the changing workforce in order to provide insight and guidance as a business coach. I focused specifically on acquiring a deep appreciation for the kind of leader who was most effective in harnessing the greatest of the uniqueness of today's workforce. What I discovered during the research process was that radical changes were taking place in the workforce. These changes involve gender, generations, and geography. Along with cost cutting and economic pressures that have resulted in downsizings, rightsizings, and mergers and acquisitions, these changes have resulted in disconnected employees.

I also discovered that despite the annual report of *Fortune's* 100 Best Companies to Work For (companies that had made significant progress in creating a work environment where the employees and the employer win), plenty of companies had not made any changes to their culture or leadership style to accommodate the new workforce. Today's workforce is a melting pot, yet many of the cultures in corporate America are still rooted in beliefs and values that were designed by and for the white male. In my interviews I found many senior leaders who recognized the need for change but did not know how to go about facilitating that change. As I pulled more data and engaged in more interviews, I found that I had a burning desire to find a way to make the connection. The companies that have made adjustments in leadership styles and cultures have experienced positive change and are growing, so why aren't more companies making this effort?

Throughout my years in corporate America I engaged in an ongoing dialogue with anyone who would listen about the "old model of leadership" needing to evolve. I don't know if anything was ever solved during those conversations, but what I held on to was that leadership behaviors and values were going to have to change in order for passion to be restored, for authentic relationships to be developed, and for the workforce to become inspired again.

I have long been a student of change and leadership. My personal commitment to help people develop serves as the inspiration behind the writing of this book. I believe with every fiber in my body that leaders have the awesome responsibility of helping others realize their full potential. Throughout this book you will see references to many famous management/leadership gurus, such as John P. Kotter, Warren Bennis, and Peter Drucker. You will also see references to twenty-first-century cutting-edge leadership researchers such as Marcus Buckingham. There are also references to a lot of good leaders who are not so famous. Why? Because some of the best leadership lessons I have learned were not obtained in the corporate environment. They were obtained from the school of life. These life lessons have taught me the importance of valuing differences, of building relationships, and of connecting with people.

So what is this book about? It's about developing a new leadership style that is capable of transforming corporate America in order to optimize the twenty-first-century workforce. It has been written to serve as a roadmap for anyone who is serious about harnessing the best of what I believe is every company's greatest asset: its people.

There is a good amount of data included in this book; it has been written that way intentionally. I recognize from my own experience as a former senior corporate executive that to build a business case for change, you've got to paint a vision that is based upon evidence—you've got to be able to quote the facts. So to those who share this belief, you'll have a field day gaining better knowledge about the changing workforce.

This book also contains a tremendous amount of practical advice to help you in your leadership development. Be forewarned: your thoughts, beliefs, philosophies, and practices will be challenged. But the challenges are for a good reason. By facing these challenges head-on, you will be taking the first step in evolving your leadership capabilities. My hope is that the discoveries you will make as a result of reading this book will be the catalyst for you to make the choice as a leader to initiate and embrace necessary change.

I believe that the success of a leader is directly tied to his or her ability to connect with the team and inspire and develop others to achieve their greatest. In our knowledge economy, leaders must be able to foster an environment where each individual is able to contribute and feel valued and will thus support innovation and creativity. Through encouraging innovation and creativity, organizations will become capable of building new relationships with today's savvy, ever-changing consumer. Creating this kind of environment requires more than framed slogans. It requires leaders who will be advocates for behavioral change that enhances innovation.

There have been and will continue to be hundreds of books written each year about leadership. As long as there are people coming together to achieve a common goal, regardless of the industry or arena, there will be a need to examine, tweak, and evolve leadership. I believe that it is time for a new type of leader. Why? Because to harness the greatest of the most diverse workforce in history it will take a breed of leader who can create powerful connections, who can build communities of best practices that leverage individual strengths and encourage risk taking and "real-time" learning. The leader who is capable of achieving these objectives I call the Hybrid Leader. This book introduces this new leadership style. What's different about this leader? He or she blends the best of traditional masculine behaviors and values with the best of traditional feminine behaviors and values to formulate a new style that represents the most successful way to develop today's diverse workforce. This concept was created based upon my own leadership beliefs and real-life corporate experiences. In addition, throughout the book I reference research and case studies that validate and support this leadership style.

The primary goal of this book is to cause you to pause and think. I also hope that it will inspire you to become a leader who is committed to transforming corporate America into a place where people can reconnect with a passion for work. What kind of business environment will be created once the transformation is complete? A place where everyone has his or her dream job. A place where everyone is valued and appreciated for what he or she does. A place where fulfillment and prosperity fit like a hand and glove. It is a place that you can be a part of creating!

PART 1

THE PAIN

CHAPTER 1

Something Is Wrong with This Picture

*Only as high as I reach can I grow, only as far as I
seek can I go, only as deep as I look can I see, only
as much as I dream can I be.*

—Karen Ravin

Disconnected Employees

On Friday afternoons at 4:50 p.m. in offices all around this country, guess what most people are doing? They're watching the clock tick. Most people in the corporate environment are sitting at their desks just counting the nanoseconds down until they can get out of Dodge. And you know how S-L-O-W a clock moves when you are in a hurry, right? The energy level and excitement in the anticipation of a weekend is tremendous. You might say that this activity is perfectly normal, given that most people are ready for the weekend by Friday—to which I say you are right. But it is what happens on Sunday that is the big problem. Read on.

My sister Mary is one of those employees who counts the minutes until she can get off work. But her countdown time starts at 2:45 p.m. because she is a nurse working the 7 a.m. to 3 p.m. shift. Mary and I are very close. That may be due to the fact that we grew up in a small, three-bedroom house with eight other sisters and brothers. My parents were devout Catholics who didn't quite get that the rhythm method was intended to prevent pregnancy—but that's a story for another time. Knowing Mary as I do, I can honestly tell you she loves the weekend. Every Friday afternoon, it's like watching a person being released from jail. For her, life begins at three o'clock on Friday afternoon. Her excitement about the weekend is contagious, and we often end up talking until late every Friday night.

Sometimes I'll check in with her on Sundays to see how her weekend went. The person who was full of energy and excitement on Friday is not the same person I am talking to on Sunday evening.

"Girl," she says, "I'm just praying for a bad storm."

"Why?" I ask.

"So I don't have to go to work tomorrow morning. I can't stand those trippin' people. My boss gets on my last bad nerve. She's destroyed all the good nerves I once had. No one appreciates a thing that I do. I'm sick and tired of being sick and tired of that place."

She feels trapped, abused, and unappreciated. My heart goes out to her. This is what is so very sad yet so real for millions and millions of people in the United States.

"Why don't you just leave?" I ask.

Her answer is always the same: "My family and my patients need me. I'll just have to struggle on."

Let me share a startling fact with you. Don Whetmore, of the Productivity Institute, reiterates that 80 percent of all Americans wake up on Monday morning and they don't want to go to work! Let me repeat that: 80 percent of all Americans wake up on Monday morning and they don't want to go to work. People are not just a little upset about their jobs; they're very upset. In fact, a landmark study commissioned by Lluminari, Inc., and led by Dr. P. Michael Peterson, Ed.D., from the University of Delaware suggests one in three Americans may be making themselves sick just by going to work. The study shows that differences in the way men and women are managed, fueled by the differences in what they value most at work, place both genders at risk for cardiovascular problems, depression, and other diseases.

How many people you know have the Monday morning blues? Do you have your own personal experience of working in an environment that doesn't nourish or optimize you? These pervasive feelings in the workforce contribute to the astronomical loss of $312 billion per year from stress-related absences, according to the February 25, 2000, edition of *BusinessWeek* magazine. Through their absences, employees are acting out their severe discontent, unhappiness, and dissatisfaction with management. A Gallup survey of 3 million employees reveals that the U.S. working population is "29 percent engaged, 55 percent not engaged, and 16 percent actively disengaged" (HR.com). The data don't lie. It doesn't sound to me like any organization in this country is consistently getting the greatest contribution from every employee. What do you think?

"Isn't it amazing that people don't appear on the balance sheet, but they drive everything else that does?" That's exactly how Michael Holmes, the former chief human resource officer of Edward Jones, puts it. That seems to be the thing many CEOs and managers have forgotten: people and their efforts are the root of great-performing companies.

Let me tell you what is driving these problems in the workforce. The biggest contributor is poor leadership! In interviews that I have conducted and in my coaching relationships, poor leadership is consistently cited as a major cause of job dissatisfaction. Today's leaders fail to earn employee respect due to a lack of knowledge, skills, or integrity. Leaders are also intimidating, failing to show concern or build relationships with employees. This suggests to me that the current form of leadership in corporate America doesn't work anymore. It's that simple, yet that complex.

Now this is not a put-down on the leadership style that worked so well in the '50s, '60s, and '70s. Quite the contrary, the top-down, "I am in charge so do what I say" leadership style was most effective for that time, given that a great deal of the workforce was male, ex-military, and accustomed to working in that type of environment. Individuals who have been in leadership positions for some time and have experienced success will resist the notion of the need to adopt a new leadership style. You can count on it and expect it. But these changes are so badly needed in today's business environment. We know from the work conducted by Harvard professor John P. Kotter that twenty-first-century organizations will be less bureaucratic and more transparent and inclusive. We also know that men who incorporate a military style of leadership no longer dominate the workforce. Warren G. Bennis suggests that because of the changing environment, the world in which an all-powerful leader can save an enterprise no longer exists.

It Takes More Than a Paycheck

Now, in the beginning of the twenty-first century, we have the most diverse workforce that has ever been seen on the face of the earth. Global diversity is the name of this game! We have five generations in the workforce. Five! According to Workforce 2020, 75 percent of all people entering the workforce are women, minorities, or immigrants. Things are just a little different, wouldn't you say? The speed of change is incredible. Whole industries come and go overnight.

Think about these questions:

- Are you motivated by a leader who talks down to you?

- Are you motivated to perform for a leader who is only interested in himself or herself?

- Are you willing to give 100 percent to your organization when you feel you are not valued?

- Are you tired of the infighting?

- Do you want your company to be more consumer-focused?

- Are you tired of feeling like you are a commodity that gets used and discarded?

Do you agree with me that the time has come for a new style of leadership? Would you say that corporate America would benefit from a leadership style that can be the catalyst for restoring employee loyalty, pride, and dedication to quality results?

Give Me Credit for My Contributions, Would Ya, Please?

There are many significant leadership mistakes that we must recognize and accept if we want to make positive changes. Let me make myself clear. I am not saying that leaders have to be perfect. No human being is perfect. What I am saying is that there are mistakes that leaders make that can be avoided if we are willing to adopt different leadership philosophies and behaviors. For example, one reason that employees who have previously demonstrated a commitment to the organization become disconnected is because their leaders borrowed their ideas and took personal credit for work they themselves did not do. Nothing turns an employee off more than reporting to someone who has the "I" mentality instead of the "we" mentality.

In a recent conversation, I was once again reminded of the impact that a leader's lack of demonstration of the "we" mentality can have. David is a district sales manager. He reports to a female section sales director. David is one of an eight-member team that reports to this woman. He is the youngest of the group both in age and in tenure with the organization. He is hungry to add value, and he is truly an out-of-the-box thinker. He likes to challenge the status quo and come up with best practices that really make a difference. He has an entrepreneurial spirit. His section sales director recognized David's abilities and asked him to spearhead an initiative focused on retail compliance. David attacked the opportunity with vigor. He assembled a team and quickly produced a best practice that provided a process that would have an immediate, positive improvement upon the section and potentially the organization as a whole. He eagerly shared his ideas with his section sales director. She thanked him for his hard work and told him that she would submit the work to her area sales director for further testing and piloting.

David was proud of himself and his team. He immediately shared the excitement with his development team by sending out a voicemail filled with accolades. He told the team that the best practice was being forwarded to the area sales director, and that they could expect to hear some follow-up in about thirty days. About three weeks after submitting the information to his section sales director, David was perusing the company's intranet, where best-practice programs and other information are shared. With shock and utter amazement he saw the best practice that his development team introduced. His first thought was that the area sales director had approved the best practice and this was the announcement. But what he found out is that his section sales director submitted the best practice as if she had created the idea and developed the program. David was absolutely livid.

When he called me he was about two seconds from nuclear meltdown. My immediate reaction was to ask him to give her the benefit of the doubt. But as I listened to more of the story it became abundantly clear that she had stolen his idea and taken credit. She was totally focused on advancing her own career even at the expense of her team. I asked him what he intended to do about it. His response was, "Nothing. I'll just never offer up any other ideas." What a total shame. By displaying the "I" instead of the "we" mentality, the section sales director had disengaged an employee whose ideas could have represented huge synergy gains for the organization.

This is just one example, but there are a lot of bitter employees in the workforce. Some of these employees have been displaced and are angry. Others have had it with management and have mentally shut down. Still others are frustrated with the corporate giant who refuses to acknowledge employees' needs. Great leaders must recognize the situations affecting the workforce and make the adjustments needed to connect with and develop their employees. It will take compassion on the part of leaders in order to help individuals who have lost trust to rechannel their energy for the good of the employer.

If disconnected, frustrated employees and egotistical leaders are one part of the problem, the other part is the organizational culture that has been created as a result of executive leadership. I believe there are as many different cultures in an organization as there are individual leaders.

The global marketplace has reshaped corporate America, and it has become far more complex to conduct business today. Day after day you hear people talking about doing more with less. Article after article focuses on the need for employees to perform at their maximum levels. If we want employees to perform at their best, we must change the working environment so that it can happen.

Today's employees have lost trust in their organizations. Without the benefit of a relationship built on trust, it is very difficult for people to believe that any changes implemented will be to their good as well as to the profitability of the organization. This trust deficiency is undermining the realization of the full contribution of employees. According to the findings of the Trust and Effectiveness Survey conducted with 210 CEOs of companies with an average of 175 employees and a median revenue of $40 million, over 75 percent indicated that workplace trust is "extremely important" to the success of their business.

Many corporations are still operating under structures that were created in the 1970s or earlier when the business environment was primarily composed of white men, very few women, and even fewer people of different ethnic cultures altogether. Today's workforce is more diverse than ever before in our history. Each generation and each cultural background brings different experiences and varying definitions of how work fits into life.

The entire business model will be impacted by the diversity of the workforce in the twenty-first century. After all, employees are also consumers and customers. These changes in the workforce present a tremendous opportunity for corporate America, but only for those who are willing to make the adjustments needed to experience success.

Right People, Right Bus, Wrong Driver

Jim Collins, author of *Good to Great*, offers a compelling argument for any organization desiring success to be diligent about getting the right people on the bus and getting the wrong people off the bus. But what if it's the leadership that needs to be put off the bus? How do employees go about leading the charge to get rid of the people who are in charge? You can't achieve greatness if you don't have a leader who is strong and willing to create an environment where greatness can become a reality. Can employees really make a difference? Yes, to an extent.

My belief is that you can have the right people but a bad leader and get terrible results. When employees feel trapped or underappreciated, they respond to that feeling. Employees who work for a leader who they feel threatened by often retreat in an attempt to do what any human would do: protect themselves. Guy Finley's statement is most appropriate here: "Discouragement is a negative emotion with more than one trick up its dark sleeve. It tricks you into mentally or emotionally dwelling in the very place you want to leave." It takes real courage and dedication to try to make changes around a leader who is unwilling to support needed change. Later in the book, I will be giving you practical steps to embrace the hybrid leadership style. But I feel compelled to offer those of you who have read thus far some hope that will help you move from feeling trapped.

Following is a list of seven steps to take if you are willing to accept this challenge.

1. *Recognize your power of choice.* No one should ever feel

like a victim. Each of us possesses the power of choice, and, consequently, we are responsible for the outcome based on the choice we make.

2. *Build strategic alliances with leaders at higher levels within the company who support your opinions, beliefs, or philosophies.* These individuals will be able to help you with the next steps.

3. *Build a business case for your position.* Don't focus on "I feel" or "I think"; focus on the data. Find the information that will prove your change to be valuable.

4. *Build a compelling argument.* As in the previous step, use data to prove your points and be sure to show the value to the company, not just to you or your department.

5. *Communicate your positioning with conviction and confidence.* If you don't believe in your idea, who else will?

6. *Exercise some patience, and watch for changes to begin.* Be prepared to answer questions, do more research, or take on more of a leadership role in the implementation of your idea.

7. *Determine whether you or not you've been able to influence and persuade.* If yes, great; if not, you are back to step 1. Are you willing to try again?

Leaders can fall anywhere within the spectrum of doing most everything right to doing most everything wrong. You must choose what kind of leader you want to be, and also what kind of leader you want to follow.

The pain will not go away without intentional changes being made in corporations throughout America. The pain is real and the impact is profound.

CHAPTER 2

The Impact of the Pain

*Progress occurs when courageous, skillful leaders seize
the opportunity to change things for the better.*

—Harry S. Truman

The Cost of the Problem

To truly solve workplace problems, we must totally understand the source of the problems. In this chapter, we focus on just that: understanding the problems. It is important to note that my focus is on problems experienced in the business world. But we can't fool ourselves. When employees have problems in their professional lives, it affects every other facet of their lives as well. In fact, many times employees who feel trapped and unable to express their dissatisfaction in the work environment often take out their feelings on their loved ones. Some turn to drugs, alcohol, or other things even worse to numb the pain. The problems and frustrations we all face in our business compromise our ability to experience a fulfilled life.

Employees who are disconnected may express their feelings in the following ways:

- They show up physically, but they are checked out mentally.

- They stop thinking about the business as an entrepreneur.

- They move into a robotic mentality.

- They make more mistakes.

- They treat customers badly because they feel they are being treated badly.

- Their emotional intelligence levels are down, and often there are expressions of anger. (This is one of the biggest influencing factors relating to violence in the workplace.)

Nothing in this list supports enhanced productivity. We must understand that there is a price to pay for the pain that the workforce is feeling. The Gallup organization has conducted extensive research that can help anyone understand the staggering price that organizations pay for disconnected employees. The Gallup research estimates that disengaged workers cost employers between $292 billion and $355 billion a year. It's unthinkable!

Not gaining insight and understanding of the problems that result in companies paying a high price will seriously affect the ability of any organization or team to experience short- and long-term success. This alone should be the catalyst for making a course correction and taking action. If that's not enough, think about the cost of turnover, both tangible and intangible. In the knowledge economy in which we find ourselves, organizations cannot afford costly turnover. According to a Society of Human Resource Management article, the U.S. Labor Department has predicted a skilled-labor shortage by 2010. There simply won't be enough workers with the right skills to staff the nation's needs. I make this point throughout the book because many organizations have not accepted this information as truth and therefore have done nothing to proactively address recruiting and retention strategies.

All for One and One for One: Are We on the Same Team?

American Airlines, the largest airline in the world, has been on the brink of bankruptcy for some time. A major contributing factor was the drastic reduction in corporate and personal travel after the terrorist attacks on September 11, 2001. To avoid bankruptcy, CEO Don Carty and his executive team appealed to all of the various unions, including the flight attendants and pilots, to accept a pay cut totaling $620 million (NBC5.com, April 21, 2003). Carty explained that the company's survival depended on the total commitment of the entire team. "We will either succeed together or fail together" was the mantra. In a historical vote, every one of the unions elected to honor the company's request to take a pay cut. It seemed that American Airlines would be able to dodge the bankruptcy bullet after all.

Unfortunately, word got out that although the vast majority of American Airlines employees' paychecks would be reduced, a certain elite group of executives would not only maintain their current pay levels but would also receive bonuses. As this information became public, there was much disappointment and disgust. Many people had looked to Don Carty as the leader who would be able to navigate the organization to avoid bankruptcy. Carty's gross misjudgment of the impact that endorsing the bonuses would have left many wondering about his trustworthiness and his leadership. As one AA pilot said, "It will be a long time before we can trust him or his senior executive team. We can no longer take for granted that they will do the right thing for all of us."

How could these executives think that it would be okay for people making hundreds of thousands of dollars less than them to make a sacrifice but not them? These executives suffered from the "ME, MYSELF, AND I" disease.

I attribute it to ego, lack of connection, and lack of understanding of the true meaning of leadership. Have you been in

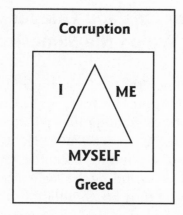

situations like this? Do you know people who have had similar experiences? The answer, unfortunately, is probably yes. And how did it make you feel? Did it make you want to give more or do more for the company? I doubt it. In fact, in the interviews I've conducted, people who felt like they were being treated "less than" showed up to work physically, but their hearts were not there. They got their jobs done but nothing more. The human spirit wants to do good. In fact, we have a yearning to fulfill our destinies. But when confronted with challenges we don't understand and can't process, we fall into a defensive posture.

The impact of downsizing, rightsizing, mergers, and acquisitions has caused a fracture to occur in the relationship between organizations and employees. Employee loyalty is fragile at best. A recent Fast Company survey revealed that people leave companies not because of the organization but because of its leaders. Some say that the downsizing and rightsizing over the past several years has left the workforce feeling resentful. Companies who have had to downsize have done so under the mind-set that it would make them more competitive and widen the margins, thereby increasing profitability. This message hasn't been well received by the workforce, who watches senior executives be dismissed with million-dollar packages. In fact, it has created disconnected and disgruntled employees. This disconnect has resulted in decreased commitment and motivation. For many employees it has been the source of a new survival mentality that has negatively impacted productivity. Organizations have been so focused on profitability at any cost that they have forgotten what's behind the numbers. And what's behind the numbers is people.

It would be unfair and less than honest for me to say that I or anyone else has a magical answer to what's wrong with corporate America. Some say that greed has overtaken doing what's right. For sure, that's part of it. There has been a huge amount of attention paid to corporate scandals recently, and rightfully so. In our society, the presumption goes, good kids grow up to be good adults, and good adults do the right thing. Unfortunately, this isn't always the case, as the last few years have demonstrated. Good people get confused or stressed and make bad decisions. When you are a CEO who makes bad decisions, it affects a lot of lives other than your own. Investors are starting to take a bold stand against unethical behaviors and are sending a very loud message to corporate America. That message is, "Something is very wrong."

Silos, Turf Wars, and Infighting

Futurist Warren Evans says, "Successful businesses of the twenty-first century will leverage every alliance and network." I believe he is right, and I believe that this extends to the inside of each and every company. In organizations where cross-functional teams don't exist, what you'll find are silos. Silos are created when everyone works in their own department with little if any connection to other departments. In a day and time when every company is looking for increased profitability, it is unthinkable that breaking down the silos wouldn't be the first area of focus. Think about how much money is wasted because of a lack of coordination and communication. Think about how much time is wasted because of turf wars. Isn't the enemy supposed to be on the outside?

A few weeks ago I was coaching a friend who recently joined a very large consumer goods organization. He was sharing with me his disappointment that the division of the organization in which he worked had no returned-goods policy. I asked if any other part of the organization had a policy. He said he thought that several other divisions had a returned-goods policy, but that they weren't willing to share the information.

"Does the company believe in best practices?" I asked. He started laughing. "That would be too much like doing what was right," he said.

Each division was competing against the other divisions. There's no motivation for anyone to break down the walls between the sister companies. What a shame. This is an example of profits being stolen from the inside.

Another example of the negative impact of silos came to me while coaching another client. She had discovered that three different departments had purchased the exact same data from an outside source at a cost of approximately $150,000 for each purchase.

"How did this happen?" I asked.

She responded, "No one knows what's happening within other departments."

"What about the department heads?" I asked. "Don't they review budgets together? No? Okay, what about the vice president they report to? Doesn't he or she review the budget expenditures?"

"Well, the truth of the matter," she said, "is that each one of the heads of the department wants to be first to come up with a leading new capability. This data is going to help them do that. So they are actually in a race and won't share information with each other. They intentionally bury expense items like this so that their colleagues won't know what they are working on."

I don't want to sound like a broken record, but isn't the competition the enemy? Why waste all of this time, energy, and effort playing these kinds of games? This is not good leadership behavior. This is poor leadership behavior. It is negative and wasteful. It needs to stop!

The Negative Impact of Personal Agendas

Don't get me wrong. Leaders should debate. They should be able to disagree. They should be able to run their own departments, but not at the expense of advancing the business because they are busy advancing their own agendas. Everyone knows that a leader's responsibility is to perform well, and sometimes better than well. But if you are doing it by stepping on a member of your own family, shame on you!

Every leader in any position is focused on keeping the boss happy so that he or she can keep the next level happy so that the executives can keep the stockholders happy. This is just another part of the leadership business game. But sometimes a leader's strong desire to meet expectations that are unrealistic without a willingness to challenge those expectations can get him or her into trouble. The result is that employees begin to see a cloud of doubt floating above their heads, which has a terribly negative impact on trust.

Let me paint a picture of how personal agendas and silos negatively impact communication and ultimately productivity. One of my clients just recently went through an integration process. Her company was acquired by an international organization, and the impact of the acquisition was starting to become a reality. The problem was that the culture of the acquiring organization was drastically different from the culture that my client's team was accustomed to. My client was very comfortable with planning budgets a year in advance. The acquisition slowed down the budget planning process. As a result, the year began and the field sales teams were not provided with budget information, but they were told to set up programs as usual. Being dedicated employees, the sales team sold programs for the first six months based upon the previous year's budget allocation.

Unfortunately, when the budgets were finally distributed, the amounts were quite a bit lower than anticipated. Any programs that had been sold that the budget did not cover had to be withdrawn. The sales team was extremely frustrated by this activity but initially put forth the effort to rearrange promotional programs in order to meet the budget expectations. Yet another change was made less than two weeks after the budget adjustments had been communicated to the accounts by the sales team. The team was so negatively impacted by this action that they started to distrust the validity of all the information coming out of the home office. One employee said, "Well, I'll just wait two weeks since I can't trust the head office people to get it right, and I know it will change anyway."

During that two-week time period while the account executive was waiting for verification of promotional information, the competition locked up promotional time slots. His company was eliminated from any opportunities to promote their products for the next two months. Now ask yourself these questions: How do you think the client account feels about the performance and abilities of this organization? Do you think that the company's performance was affected? The simple answer, yes. In fact, the company had to engage in creative inventory management (better known as "loading") at the end of the year in order to make their annual sales numbers.

We must challenge ourselves to understand why these situations occur. How could this situation have been handled differently? Would better direction from the leaders have helped? I think so. When employees are connected through clear and consistent communication, even when things go wrong they are supportive and productive. But the communication must be consistent, and it must be transparent. In this case there was not only inconsistent communication but incorrect communication. Duplication of efforts, missed opportunities and disconnected employees are the price that is paid.

The Business World Is Looking
for a Few Good Leaders

Older, established companies are likely to have CEOs at the helm who can't relate to the needs and desires of today's workforce. The problem is that CEOs who have not been sensitized to the changing world still believe that outdated policies and procedures—such as rigid work schedules, private networks, and nepotism—still work today. They don't work today! In the good old days, as some would call them, people showed up to work leaving behind the problems that they were facing in their private lives. In fact, I can clearly remember one of my managers in the late '80s saying something to the team like, "Check your problems at the door. You are now here to work." Employees cannot check part of themselves at the door. How ridiculous! Employees must be respected in totality.

Companies that have long histories have been slow to recognize and adjust to the changes that are occurring in the workplace. As a result, many of them are struggling to incorporate behaviors and policies that will help maintain the company's competitive edge. This is rather ironic given the mantra to do more with less, to give it your all, to be fully engaged. If these are sincere desires, then why the struggle to make changes that will make this become a truism? What I have discovered is that the most senior leaders at the top are clueless as to the problems. Therefore, it is virtually impossible for them to teach or motivate the middle level of management to do anything different than what they are doing now. CEOs need to get educated. I respectfully challenge any CEO who is reading this book to find three employees in your company who you know will give you the truth, and ask them about the realities they face working for the company on a daily basis. If you can get the truth, it will shock you. But it will also open the door for you to take action that can fuel phenomenal success for the organization.

Now I recognize that the aforementioned statements generalize CEOs. Some organizations are headed by CEOs who do get it. What I discovered in my research was that the CEOs who do get it have had some personal experience that has changed their lives. They know of another CEO who has been fired, or they have children who are about to enter the work environment, or they have visited others parts of the world and are able to see things in a completely different perspective.

My sister Amberosine was recently diagnosed with breast cancer. She has completed her surgeries and chemo treatments. The chemo treatments proved themselves to be more difficult that she had forecasted. In fact, she thought she would be right back to work after the surgery. Things didn't work out that way. The chemo left her sick and weak. She works for a newspaper and reports to the general manager. When she explained to him her inability to work, he didn't hesitate to support her. He said, "My wife and the CEO's wife have both had similar experiences. We know how difficult it is. And we want you to know that you are valued and we support you. So don't worry about coming in to work. When you feel like you can do something, do it from home. When you don't feel like it, then don't do anything. We want you back when you are ready to come back, and we eagerly await that day. But there is no pressure. And you don't have to worry about your job being here when you return."

Wow! Can I tell you how much this approach to her problem meant to her and to our family? It has meant everything. Would her manager and the CEO be so supportive if they themselves had not had similar experiences? I do not know, but I do know this: when you can relate to someone else's challenges and pains, it makes you more empathetic. It is important to demonstrate empathy even if you haven't personally experienced what your employees have. It lets your employees know that you are listening to them and that you are concerned for them on a personal level.

When I began gathering data on benchmark companies, I decided that it would be helpful to carefully examine what was different in these companies versus the companies that had made the "100 Best Companies to Work For" listings. After comparing benefits, market share, turnover, and customer satisfaction levels, as well as other factors, I found the key difference to be that in the cases of the companies that were viewed as "employers of choice," major change had taken place. The changes in these companies were driven by the CEOs' open support for creating a work environment where people wanted to come to work and give their absolute best. When a CEO says, "We must make changes and here is why, and here is the benefit to you personally and to the organization," employees respond, but it has to be more than lip service.

When the CEO only provides lip service, policies are put into place but everyone knows they don't mean a thing. I personally know of several companies that have CEOs who have endorsed flexible work schedules. But because there is no role modeling of this at the top, when employees ask about being able to create a flexible work schedule they are told that the flexible work schedule policy is only for people who don't want to get promoted. In other words, "If you do it, your chances of advancement in this company are over." Are the policies that your organization has established to embrace the employee in totality meaningful or not? Take a reality check. See if any of your senior leaders are granting the use of this policy. How about interviewing employees to ascertain how effective the policy truly is?

Challenging the old way of doing things is more than a notion. There is a certain amount of fear that has to be overcome in order for employees to find the courage to drive change within the organization. I recently helped several female clients make a business case for inclusion, female leadership, and diversity. It was quite a challenge. The company has not experienced drastic turnover, although turnover has been on the climb for the last several years. So we couldn't use that as a part of the business case. Instead, we had to look for other benefits that would make senior leadership want to support this initiative. The company is number one in its market and has been extremely profitable. But—and it's a big but—there are no minority leaders above the director level. Women and minorities are underutilized throughout the organization. The CEO has no motivation to make any changes; he will be retiring in the next few years. The senior VPs don't want to rock the boat because they want to be at the top of the list for the president position, thinking that the president would take the CEO position upon the CEO's retirement. The prospect of any change in this corporate structure wasn't too promising.

Nonetheless, we continued our pursuit, and indeed we made a minimal level of progress. We raised the awareness of the underutilization of females in the organization, and we inspired the women to be more vocal. But we didn't achieve our target. Why? We didn't have the CEO's or president's open endorsement of the value of the work. Even though the CEO has an area on the scorecard that called out the importance of diversity and developing women leaders for the future, there was no action being taken. And you know what? There won't be either. Until the CEO openly states that he is committed to this initiative, it will only be a vision that goes nowhere. So you might be saying, "If everyone is a leader, then why does the burden rest with the CEO?" The burden rests at the top because the person at the top sets the tone for the organization. This is part of the deal for becoming a CEO. The vision was there, but obviously it wasn't enough. I love the way Joel Barker puts it: "Vision without action is merely a dream. Action without vision just passes the time. Vision with action can change the world."

Command-and-Control Leadership Wrapped in Egos

If organizations are serious about experiencing success, then they must challenge everything about the current way they develop their leaders. This includes the leadership tenets that drive the development of the next generation of leaders. Current leaders must be held accountable for leadership behavior that reflects a commitment to the new tenets. For some organizations this even means taking on a chairman of the board who is still holding on to old theories. Organizations must be able to develop leaders who understand that success is the result of nurturing the passion, commitment, and creative energy of the organization. It is only through these efforts that organizations will be able to remain innovative and produce high-quality products and services. That means not just talking about empowering employees, but doing it. You know, I honestly believe that there are leaders who are afraid that if their employees become empowered, then their job will not be needed. What a thought!

A lot of the senior leaders in corporate America have egos the size of the world. Egos get in the way of making needed change. Some people actually view the use of ego as a necessary component of getting to the top. I disagree. Recently one of my clients was promoted to vice president. At that time she was told that she needed to let go of interfacing with people who were not in her peer group. "You are a senior leader now, and you must maintain a certain level of separation from everyone else."

She called me because this counsel, received from her manager, was in direct opposition to her core values. She believes that leaders need to be "real," regardless of their level within the organization. She struggled with the fact that her boss was so intent on the separation. This kind of thinking is exactly why senior executives don't know what is really happening in the company. People begin to view leadership as a title. Nothing could be further from the truth. Leadership has absolutely nothing to do with a title. Learning to balance ego with humility is critical.

When I think about leadership position and title, I think about Jesus Christ. Jesus Christ washed the feet of his disciples to demonstrate his willingness to be humble. John 13:12–16 explains his action in more detail. The essence is this: Leaders recognize their responsibility to remain humble.

There is a certain mentality among many leaders that they have earned the right to call the shots. That is wrong and deadly thinking. A leader has a responsibility to serve. The reason many leaders have developed supersized egos is that the corporate world has so greatly valued individual performance. But in the

twenty-first century, team performance, not individual performance, will represent the greatest value to an organization.

During lunch with an old client, the importance of putting
down egos became abundantly clear. I had previously coached
this client and was checking in to see how many of the behavior
changes we had made were lasting. It was interesting. She was
at complete peace despite the fact that the business was going
south.

"How are you maintaining peace in the midst of such tremendous organizational change?" I questioned.

She responded, "I see this situation for what it is, an ego
struggle for power."

Many senior leaders know that change is needed, but they
are determined to fight the needed change to the end because
they don't want to say that the model they built isn't working
anymore. How wrong is that? But how often does it happen?
Every day!

Egos are a normal part of any competitive environment,
but they are only good to the degree that they add value for
everyone. We can't hold on to those things that have lived past
their prime. Imagine if someone, anyone, was trying to tell you
that the typewriter was the most efficient invention since the
printing press. What would your response be? You would probably say the typewriter was wonderful a couple of decades ago,
but today we have technology that enables us to eliminate the
typewriter. Right? Right!

Leaders think that if they admit "their" idea no longer
works, it is an affront to them personally. So why is it that senior
leaders don't want to let go of behaviors, strategies, and beliefs
they know so well? The answer is simple. It's because they have to
learn something new. It's not their idea. It's someone else's idea.

Forget about this personal agenda stuff. Forget it! It shouldn't
matter if it's your idea or my idea. What should matter is that
the idea has benefit for the employees, the organization, and its

customers. As my mother likes to say, "When you know better, do better." We now know better!

Let's Use the Entire Workforce, Why Don't We?

The twenty-first-century employee wants to be valued but also developed. As more and more women climb the corporate ladder, they will expect the glass ceiling to be removed. If it is not, they are prepared to take the steps necessary to fulfill their professional objectives, including walking out the door. A recent Korn/Ferry survey of 425 women executives found that the main reason for leaving their old jobs was because they wanted a larger role in running a company. There is a growing and disturbing trend of women leaving big corporations to be more intimately involved in smaller companies. If this trend continues, valuable talent will be lost, and more important, valued resources to transform the leadership behaviors that no longer work will be lost.

Corporate America will have to make major adjustments in order to embrace women as leaders. Generally speaking, this has not happened. According to Fast Company, women are leaving corporate America at nearly twice the rate as men. If this trend continues, it will leave a huge knowledge gap, particularly given the predicted skilled-labor shortage. It will also have a huge negative impact upon innovation and fostering an environment where people are more connected and valued. Organizations are mistaken in thinking they can profit from a great recruiting strategy without balancing it with a great retention strategy. The continuous exit of women will make it harder and harder for organizations to attract top female candidates.

As of March 2002, only nine companies in the Fortune 500 were run by female CEOs (*WOW! Facts 2002*, Business Women's Network). Women are extremely close to making up half the workforce, but their climb up the corporate ladder continues to be rocked by an uneven playing field. We operate in the knowledge economy. What CEO would not want to leverage the intellectual brainpower of women? Women want to experience job satisfaction. This strong desire will drive them to attempt to transform their current work environments. But if the corporation doesn't respond, they are prepared to exercise their choices, including taking leadership roles in smaller companies or starting their own businesses.

It is unimaginable that companies would not want to develop the most diverse talent possible, given the diverse population of their consumer base. A woman influences 80 percent of all consumer purchases, according to Catalyst, and women are responsible for approximately 50 percent of all checks written in America. Unfortunately, there is still a perception that women are not as capable in leadership positions as men are. That is total nonsense! The sooner organizations get on board with developing women leaders, the better their chance for sustained success will be.

I remember sitting in my boss's office having a rather intense discussion about diversity. At this point in my career I was at the vice president level. I had a self-imposed sense of responsibility to help the organization develop diverse leaders at every level of the organization. We were discussing why it was good for the organization to promote more women and minorities. He jokingly said, "We have you. Isn't that enough?" But it wasn't a joke. It was coming out of his very soul. I must have looked shocked at his statement, because he asked if I understood that it was a joke. This kind of leadership needs to be removed from any position of influence. This old-school thinking is keeping some companies from experiencing higher levels of success by building diverse leadership.

I have spent the past year and a half coaching, speaking to, and interviewing people in corporate America. It's sad to say that this same type of story was repeated over and over again. This conversation with my boss took place in the late 1990s, almost 2000. My boss couldn't even talk about diversity without becoming uncomfortable, and it wasn't just diversity of gender and culture. He couldn't embrace diversity of thought. Bottom line: he didn't want to change. Most disappointing to me about the whole situation was that we were not that far apart in age or experience.

A similar situation occurred in one of my coaching relationships. Jackie had reached the director position working for a large retail operations company. She is an experienced professional in her early thirties. She, like many other employees in her age segment, knows what she wants. She wants to run a business unit within a ten-year time period. She is willing to apply herself and to take lateral moves as well as accept an international assignment in order to make her dream come true. For years she received accolades on her work performance, but no one could tell her what she needed to do in order to execute her plan. As one of the first African American females to reach the director level within her organization, she was convinced that it was possible to continue the journey and become a vice president or president of a business unit. The company that she worked for had never had a female VP in any segment of the business other than marketing.

After consulting with her mentors and counseling with me, she decided that the one person who could really help her understand what she needed to do in order to advance was the person who hired her: the CEO. When she was hired, the CEO was then the president of the company and was directly involved in her recruiting process. She went to him for guidance, advice, and counsel. Her question was extremely direct, specifically, "Do you think that there is an opportunity for me to advance to the level of vice president or president of a business unit?" His answer: "I don't see it happening for you." When she asked the CEO why, he simply told her that that there were so many people who, like her, had great experience and great education, but the competition was extremely tough, and he really couldn't in good faith give her false hope. What she believed that he was saying was this: you are not a white man, and only white men are viewed as credible leaders in this organization.

This news was tough to swallow for this MBA graduate who finished in the top five in her class. But she took it, digested it, and left the organization within three months. Her decision was directly connected to her conversation with the CEO. Part of her reasoning for leaving was linked to the need for changes in the company's culture. Jackie felt that the culture did not mirror the words of the mission statement: that being to create a culture where inclusivity is embraced.

I'm not quite sure if the CEO realized the message that Jackie's departure would send to other minorities and women throughout the organization. It wasn't positive. Several other minorities at that company are now actively engaged in job searches. There is a price to pay for losing good employees. It shows up not only in replacement and training costs but also in low morale and increased turnover. As I've mentioned before, the U.S. Labor Department has predicted a skilled-labor shortage. So why then aren't organizations willing to develop their people so that they can keep them? Why is there such a struggle to embrace diversity as a critical component of the business strategy? Why are women still having to fight to establish themselves as credible leaders? It boils down to this: people don't like to change, even when it is good. The pain points for some organizations haven't been intense enough to cause them to develop an appetite for this kind of change. If your company has not moved in this direction, don't worry. The pain will soon be great enough to stimulate change! But why wait until your company is breathing its last breath before you do something to address the problem? In my opinion, companies need to develop comprehensive, aggressive employee retention strategies. These retention strategies must continually evolve in order to address the expectations and desires of the current workforce.

I love the way former New York City Mayor Rudolph Giuliani in his book *Leadership* talks about leaders having a responsibility to develop appropriate structures for an organization. He asserts that a leader must form a team of people who bring out the best in each other and who are willing to take risks. There is no denying the workforce has changed. The question is, how many at the CEO level will step up to the plate to embrace a new leadership style? If the CEO is not willing to step up, who is prepared to lead the charge? Will it be you? If not you, who? We can either sit and complain, or we can do something about it. My purpose in writing this book is to help you do something about it.

CHAPTER 3

How Did We Get Here?

We are each of us angels with only one wing, and we can only fly by embracing one another.

—Lucretius

Understanding the Changing Workforce

What's different about the twenty-first-century workforce? Everything, from the way information is managed to the way employees approach work. In 1986, I began a sixteen-year relationship with my former employer. In conjunction with the application process a physical was required. Three days after my first day on the job I found out that I was pregnant. I agonized for nearly two months before I got up the nerve to tell my boss. I was so afraid that I would blow my advancement chances that I didn't want to tell her about the baby. How ridiculous is that? Very, but that's the way it was in the '80s. Children and work simply did not mix. Discussions about family were infrequent at best. You didn't see pictures of the family in the office. You were expected to arrive at work and become the property of whoever was signing the check. There were no negotiations about salary or benefits. And there wasn't anything called a signing bonus!

Workplace programs are being designed at a rapid pace in an attempt by corporations to try to meet the new demands of the workforce. It seems so simple and so commonsensical, yet the vast majority of employers resist the opportunity to build relationships with their employees based upon their current needs rather than the model from the '70s. The following grid clearly depicts the mind-set changes for today's workforce.

WHAT'S OUT	WHAT'S IN
I'm happy to have a job	I'm happy to have a job here as long as I am happy here
Tell me what to do	Give me the general scope of my responsibilities and let me demonstrate my talents
I am willing to make multiple moves at the company's request	I'll move only if it fits in with my life's plans
My family responsibilities are hidden	I want open discussions about work/life balance
I am willing to work ninety hours a week if that's what it takes to get the job done	I am willing to work extra (when it's needed for crunch projects), but I don't want to make it a habit
Physical offices	Virtual teams
I don't really care who I work for. Give me my orders so I can execute	I want to work for a leader who I can develop a relationship with, trust, and respect
Snail mail	Fax, e-mail, Palm Pilots, Blackberries
Narrowly Defined Diversity	Full inclusion with a place for everyone

The list goes on. The differences are even more pronounced depending upon the age of the employee.

The twenty-first-century workforce is experiencing radical change. These changes include growing numbers of Hispanics, African Americans, and Asians entering the workforce. The workforce composition also includes Generations X and Y and the Sandwich Generation (adults who are young enough to have children at home but old enough to have responsibility for elderly parent care). According to the U.S. Department of Labor, 70 percent of new jobs in the workforce by 2008 will be held by women and people of color. By the year 2006, Hispanics will constitute a greater percentage of the workforce than African Americans (Workforce Economic Trends). According to the Northeastern University Center for Labor Market Studies, during the 1990s new immigrants accounted for half of the increase in the U.S. workforce, and this trend is expected to continue into the early part of the twenty-first century.

Today's employees are not afraid to openly express the fact that they choose where they work. Employees have more choices than ever before as it relates to selling their skills. The belief that job security doesn't exist anymore is driving this attitude. It is translating into a trend of more workers embracing a concept of "free agency," or working wherever they will be most appreciated and where their needs and desires will best be met. According to *Time* magazine, nearly 33 percent of American workers—34 million people—are contingency workers, including temps, part-timers, consultants, freelancers, and self-employed workers.

In order to keep their employees, companies must become a resource in helping their employees deal with all of the realities of life, inclusive of new developments such as elder care. Kimberly-Clark has a database that provides sitter service information and elder care information. According to a 1999 survey conducted by Hewitt Associates of 1,020 major U.S. employers, the percentage of employers offering elder care assistance has grown from 24 percent in 1994 to 47 percent in 1999. Given the changing dynamics of the workforce, any organization that has not thought about providing assistance in this area will need to quickly research the key components and get a program together.

Companies will have to respect spiritual rituals that will include things such as daily prayer. We can already see this happening. Ford Motor Company has designated a room in their corporate offices that can be used for naps, prayer, or meditation. Looking to at least take notice of their employees' physical health, many companies have onsite gyms or exercise classes.

Telecommuting and job sharing have been found to be beneficial for increasing productivity. A Boston College study, "Measuring the Impact of Workplace Flexibility," found that organizations that build cultures where flexible work arrangements are offered realized a positive impact on productivity, work quality, and retention. As more emphasis is placed on finding work that has meaning and purpose, people are willing to take a chance on nontraditional work arrangements. In fact, a survey by True Careers out of Reston, Virginia, found 92 percent of employees saying that the opportunity to work from home would be a key factor in deciding if they would accept a particular job. In another study conducted by the Positively Broadband Campaign, of the participants interviewed, approximately one-third said they would take the option to telecommute over higher pay.

Finally, according to a recent study conducted by Flexible Resources with side-by-side employees on flexible schedules and their managers, more than half the employees said that they were more results-oriented, and 92 percent of their managers said they were just as promotable as those who were on traditional schedules. Where does your company stand on these dramatic but real landscape changes? How are your leaders responding? One practical way of gaining a better understanding of the changes is to talk to your employees. Ask them what problems or challenges they face in their pursuit of experiencing personal and professional success.

If you are a single parent of young children, day care is a high priority. If you are in the job market and close to deciding on an employer, would you pick one that has onsite day care or one that does not? The answer seems fairly obvious, yet so many companies still don't provide onsite day care centers. One person I interviewed told me that the company-offered day care is what enables her to work until 6:45 p.m. when she has to. "Without the onsite day care I would be forced to leave work at 5:00 p.m. to get to any other day care by 6:00 p.m., and that would cause me more stress than it's worth. I need to work for a company that can accommodate my needs."

As a leader, you will have to help the organization understand that employees who ask for or even demand these types of benefits are committed, dedicated employees. It used to be that if an employee talked about anything other than work, he or she was viewed as not being loyal or committed. That kind of thinking will result in the organization losing out on the potential to recruit and retain the top talent needed to be successful.

A couple of years ago, when my company was considering hiring an MBA graduate from Duke University, I observed firsthand this shift in the desires of the new workforce. I was interviewing a man who was twenty-three years old. When I asked him if he had any questions, he responded with the following:

1. What is the company's work/life balance policy?

2. What support would the company offer to assist his wife in her employment efforts?

3. Since the company didn't have an onsite day care center, what provisions was the company prepared to make to reimburse a portion of the monthly cost?

4. Are leaders held accountable for valuing the employees from a holistic perspective?

I was blown away. This was significant. I had never in my eighteen years of business heard a male interviewee ask these kinds of questions. At that point my hope was restored for the future of corporate America. It was a glimpse into a new world where both men and women could openly express and be accepted for the value that they place on family. It was inspiring. This twenty-three-year-old didn't get the job, not because we didn't want him, but because our company wasn't able to meet his nontraditional needs.

Highly skilled individuals who are confident in the value they bring to the table are redefining the employee/employer relationship. This group of people not only wants meaning and purpose in work and recognition of their lives outside work, they also want to work in an environment where fun is permitted and encouraged. One person I interviewed put it this way: "Why should I want to work for a company that doesn't value my needs? The relationship has to be more than a paycheck." This kind of commentary speaks volumes to the fact that the mind-set of the twenty-first-century workforce toward work and its place in life is completely changing.

A profile of a typical Generation-Xer as depicted by Corporate Leadership Council research reveals the following (www.corporateleadershipcouncil.com):

- Desire for immediate and ongoing investment in skills development

- Intolerant of barriers to promotion; want to be promoted just as soon as they are ready

- Strong desire to work in collegial work environments; gratuitous trappings of corporate settings are turnoffs

- Reluctant to move at the company's request; must see near-term personal gain

- Decides what companies to work for based upon company reputation, product line, and position on diversity and inclusion

Add to this the list of desires expressed by women whom I interviewed:

- I want to work where I am valued.

- I will exercise my option to leave if I perceive that the organization is not truly committed to developing female senior executives.

- I want to work for an organization that understands and respects my desire for personal and professional success.

- I don't want to conform to the male leadership model; give me credit for being a leader who leads differently than the men.

- Level the playing field; make mentors and sponsors available to me.

- Don't look at me as though I'm the problem.

- Let me control my own destiny.

For the purposes of understanding the extent of these dramatic shifts, let's look at the perspectives of other groups within the workforce.

Older Employees

- I don't have to leave when I'm fifty-five years old.

- Organizations need to recognize the experience and wisdom of older workers and not just focus on developing the younger workers.

- Some of these younger employees don't know how lucky they have it to have so much freedom.

- I'm trying to get the hang of this change thing; be patient with me.

- I've given my life to this work. Won't somebody show me some appreciation?

White Males

- Everyone one else seems to be getting special support. What about me?

- I'm being held back now because I'm a white man.

- Everyone is telling me to relate to others, but who understands my needs?

- America's business model was built by white men and a lot of good things happened as a result of our leadership, but now we're the bad guys.

- I want to stay true to myself and advance in the company without having to play the "good ol' boy" game.

African Americans

- Organizations are still only giving lip service to including us.

- We haven't made it as black people, and now we are losing our voice in the inclusion of all minorities.

- It's harder for black men to make progress in the business world because white men feel threatened by black men.

- It is the most difficult thing in the world for a white woman to understand what a black woman experiences in corporate America.

Asians

- Just because I'm Asian does not mean that I want to work in IT or that I am used to working long hours.

- Don't assume that I live by old Asian cultures. I'm from America, too.

Hispanics

- I'm a Hispanic female with aspirations and dreams like everyone else.

- Don't assume just because I am Hispanic that means I don't speak English.

- Every person of Latin descent does not share the same culture.

- Don't judge my intellectual capabilities by my accent. I happen to speak two (or more) languages.

Other Minorities

- All Indians are not from India.

- I thought when the market became global that it included everyone on the globe.

- We're not cheap labor.

- We have innovative ideas that shouldn't be discounted just because we may not be Americans.

When you add together all of these perspectives you can see why there is a sense of urgency to develop leadership behavior that can extract potential from all these different work groups. But it doesn't stop there. How many people from other countries work in the United States? A lot. So what do they want?

- Not to be put down because they English is not their first language

- Respect for the rituals, beliefs, and values of their native countries

- To feel welcomed

- To understand how to work in this culture

Indeed, everything is different about the twenty-first-century workforce. Today's employees know what they want, and they will seek to work for the organization that will give them just that—no ifs, ands, or buts.

Diversity Redefined in Twenty-first-Century Language

It is important to understand that diversity for the twenty-first-century workforce is not limited to differences in race or gender or even age. Though most of corporate America is still stuck on thinking that diversity means black or white, male or female, it is so much more than that. Diversity must be thought of in its broadest sense and include different business environments; differing approaches to the business; different communication styles; different life experiences; differing visions, religions, benefit needs, martial status, gender, ethnicity, and so on. Diversity is all about valuing the uniqueness of each and every individual. In other words, you can be in a room of all white men or all black women and still have diversity.

I'm certainly not trying to minimize affirmative action. Affirmative action has been the catalyst for many companies to do what they should have already done without a law being passed to make them do it. Rather, I am focused on helping you understand that the context in which you use diversity is affected by a lot of different factors. These factors serve to influence whether you embrace diversity as a great part of life or see it as a necessary evil.

Companies that develop diverse talent gain a competitive advantage in pursuing their end customers. We know also that there is richness in diversity. So what don't we know? We don't know why some companies heed the call and take action because they see the writing on the wall and others don't. I honestly believe that it comes down to fear—specifically, fear of something different and fear of the unknown. Isn't it ironic that leaders preach the importance of thinking outside the box, but if your actions are outside the box, they can't handle it?

Every company should have a role that is responsible for managing diversity, but I don't think that it should be called the "diversity manager" or even "vice president of diversity." I think it should be called "vice president of organizational culture." After all, if diversity is about valuing the uniqueness of each employee, it will be through the culture of the organization that it will become a way of life, not through diversity programs. I also think that positioning this function in this light will help the organization understand the value and true meaning behind diversity and inclusion efforts. This person should be included on the executive board and should have the same level of credibility and input as the vice president of finance.

Top companies realize the importance of creating an environment where the richness of this new workforce can be optimized. According to the U.S. Department of Labor, major changes will occur in the business world that will translate into new career paradigms. The inclusion of multiple generations, differing ethnic groups, virtual teams, and many other sources of diversity are changing the face of the workforce in America and in the world.

One of my clients asked me to help him understand what changes would need to be made to his company's culture in order for the organization to be viewed as a "good place to work." Knowing what I understood the culture to be, my response was: "You've got to do something that sends a visual signal to the employee base that there is a reason that people should want to work for your company. First you need to develop leaders who can foster an environment where people feel valued and inspired to work. Second, create affinity groups so that people of different backgrounds feel like they have support for the unique challenges they face in the work environment. Then you've got to bring life to the work/life balance policy. You've got to embrace women leaders. You've got to . . ."

"Stop!" he said. "That sounds like a very long process."

"The process itself isn't long," I responded, "but changing people's minds and hearts will take more than a few training classes or videos. If you are serious about being considered a top employer, then you and your leadership will have to understand that the workforce has changed and respond to that change."

I gave him a fact sheet to stimulate his thinking process. Let me share it with you:

- By 2006, the number of jobs in the United States will be approximately 151 million, yet there will only be 141 million people in the workforce.

- One-third of all workers were fifty years of age or older by the year 2000.

- The Hispanic population is expected to reach 16 percent of the total U.S. population by 2020.

- The African American population is expected to reach 12.9 percent of the total U.S. population in 2020, up from 11.5 percent in 1980.

- The industries at the highest risk for labor shortfalls are government, energy, manufacturing, and health care. Women and minorities currently make up a large percentage of this workforce.

- The learning curve that results from the need to transfer knowledge will take its toll on productivity.

- As of the year 2000, women and minorities represented 62 percent of the U.S. workforce and 80 percent of all new workforce entries.

- Career preferences have dramatically changed for new employees thirty years of age and younger.

- Forty percent of the workforce is unmarried.

- Twenty-seven percent of single parents are men.

- One in five parents who works is single.

- As of 2002, only 38 percent of the workforce was male

Caucasian. This segment of the workforce is no longer dominant.

- The percentage of Americans over sixty-five in the work-force will have risen from 12.5 percent in 1992 to 16.5 percent by 2020.

Speaking of workers over sixty-five, approximately 61 million Americans will retire over the next thirty years. Where is the talent to take over their jobs? Employment Policy Foundation president Ed Potter states that within the next five years, the demand for labor will begin to exceed supply. Without changes to policies that guide the workplace and its employees, the nation will be unable to maintain its historic rate of economic growth. Companies and leaders have got to wrap their minds around what these trends mean in terms of the business model and the culture.

Much emphasis is placed on diversity in most companies, at least on paper. But if you were to ask each senior executive for his or her personal view of diversity, most would not be able to provide an honest answer. They probably could repeat what is included in the policies and procedures manual, but it wouldn't be an answer that comes from the heart, shaped by their beliefs and values. Until all employees commit to searching their souls and exorcising their demons about differences, diversity, and inclusion—or whatever you want to call it—it will never reach the level where it becomes a part of the fabric of the organization. Never!

I'm More Than Just an Employee

The 1990s were indeed a decade of discovery. Many of us learned that there is no such thing as job security. We also learned that there is something called information overload. We found out that we don't like being so serious all the time, and we finally gained the wisdom that money doesn't mean total happiness. I personally found out that fun is more valuable than I thought. I also faced the reality that I was missing precious time with my family as a result of my aggressive desire to experience professional success. Enter something we call work/life balance. Most of the baby boomers, like me, learned that this thing called health is truly important. Many of us learned that PDAs, computers, Blackberries, and the like don't equate to being more productive. They translate into being more accessible, hence the blurring of personal and professional time.

Everyone seems to be on the hunt for more time. There is a lot of information and evidence suggesting that, in general, Americans are looking for ways to simplify and better enjoy their lives. Employees want to find a better balance between their personal and professional lives. People want to spend quality time doing things that are important. Relationships have become far more important to people as more and more are growing up in broken homes. The newest generations of workers want more than financial compensation. They have a strong desire to experience a "full" life. Work is certainly a part of that full experience, but so are a lot of other activities. Long gone are the days when a company says, "Jump," and the employee responds, "How high?"

Employees are beginning to question how they are defined. Is there something more important than the job? Yes! In Rick Warren's *The Purpose-Driven Life*, we learned that in order for us as humans to optimize our contribution to this world, we must find purpose. The truth is, most of us don't take the time or don't know how to go about gaining an in-depth understanding of our purpose. Not being connected to one's purpose is a significant reason that there are so many unhappy people. Remember the statistics that I shared in the first chapter? I think that a lot of people are in the wrong jobs, doing the wrong things, hoping for the best. If leaders could help employees to connect with their purpose and passion, the result would be overwhelmingly positive.

I recently worked with a wonderful female executive, Lisa. Lisa works for a financial organization as a senior consultant.

As a part of the coaching process, I asked Lisa many questions about her childhood. Her answers revealed a lot. In fact, I came to understand that because of several tragedies that occurred in her childhood, Lisa had assumed an overwhelming desire to pursue a career that would afford her financial independence. Her parents divorced when she was young. She saw her mother deal with the challenges of raising children and not having the support of a total family unit. When I probed a little more to help Lisa get the purpose/passion alignment, I found out that Lisa loves sports. Her secret dream was to be a basketball coach. She's obviously not living her dream. Why? Lisa has a self-imposed perception of what she needs to do professionally in order for the world to view her as successful, and she is anchored to the need of financial independence. Lisa does excellent work as a financial consultant. But her heart longs to do something else. Lisa is an example of where a lot of people find themselves. I'm not by any means suggesting that Lisa quit her great day job to pursue her dream to become a sports coach. Instead Lisa might find a way to get involved in sports as a volunteer. And, if Lisa's company would sponsor her involvement, a win/win situation could be created. Lisa would feel valued holistically and as a result would become more engaged and loyal to her company.

Employee Skills Not Being Optimized? Go Figure

It is sad but true: employees are not being utilized to their greatest potential. One of my clients is a vice president responsible for a private label for a major manufacturer. She was promoted only after making the decision to approach the CEO of the company to make a proposal for her position to be upgraded. Her strategy was fairly straightforward. She gets calls from headhunters at least twice a month. She is known in the industry for having extraordinary customer relationship management skills. She has sold ten times the salary that she has and will ever receive from the company if she stays until retirement.

The company's ability to capture market share and build critical business relationships in accounts that she isn't even responsible for is directly tied to who she is as a professional and as a person. She is connected!

She has felt for some time that she deserved the vice president title. Her opinion was not based solely on the fact that she is a star performer. Rather, she believed that the scope of her responsibility warranted a VP title. Also, her external counterparts who worked for the competition carried the VP title. One other important point: her accounts continued to tell her that they wanted to be called by a senior leader who could make decisions on the spot. All of this combined convinced her that she deserved the title. This lady is awesome! She knows that she can add value to any organization. After carefully thinking through her proposal, she presented it to the CEO and was appointed to the vice president position.

Today's savvy workforce is not afraid to say, "Play me or trade me." The new generation of workers is getting in the face of corporate America like no generation ever before in history, even in a tough economy. Today's workforce asks a lot of questions and expects a lot of feedback. They are also much better at problem solving than the previous generations, as they have grown up using multiple data sources and technology. They want to be challenged, and if they aren't, they are out the door. "So what?" you might be thinking. "Employee turnover is a part of the game." Yes, it is. But don't forget about the predicted skilled-labor shortage and the fact that we operate in a knowledge economy. When your top talent walks out the door, there is a really good chance that he or she will end up working for the competition. When they leave, the knowledge leaves and the fallout begins. Are you ready to deal with this situation?

The Hay Group, a Philadelphia management consultant company, surveyed workers to measure their commitment. The survey results revealed that the gap between employees planning to stay at least five years and those planning to leave within the year was the largest when it came to the opportunities they were given to learn new skills. This suggests a direct relationship between learning and opportunity for advancement and employee retention.

Risk Takers Arise

The twenty-first-century workforce is also made up of risk takers. They are not afraid to leave the corporate environment and do their own thing. It is a well-known fact that the growth that has been occurring for the last few years in the U.S. economy has been fueled not by corporate America but by small business. Why are so many businesses popping up everywhere? A lot of these businesses were created as a result of downsizing, but another contributing factor is the notion that people don't want to work in bureaucratic, political environments anymore. I myself am a classic example.

In May 2000 I went to my company's CEO and said that I was burned out from traveling 80 percent of the time. I was tired of beating my head against the good ol' boy wall, carrying the torch for a new culture. I had been a vice president for five years at that point. I was the only woman and the only minority, and no one except for me seemed to care about creating a culture that was inclusive. I asked for a package and was fortunate enough to get one. I wanted out because I didn't feel valued, I didn't feel accepted, and I was tired of walking on eggshells.

When I returned home after getting off the plane, I made the decision that I still wanted to find a way to influence the change of corporate America, despite the fact that I was no longer part of it. I was concerned how it would be when my children arrived in the corporate world. I didn't want them to experience what I experienced. Prior to my leaving the organization, I had engaged in a tremendous amount of research to gain a better understanding of the trends. I had also taken the time to think about the parts of my job that made me the happiest. I knew that I had experienced all the politics I cared to for a long while. I was tired of watching the daily backstabbings. I was even more tired of trying to convince the good ol' boys that their "club" was going to damage the business. So I, like many others, started my own business.

I could have gone to another company, but I was convinced that I could serve better from the outside. I wanted to be a part of creating a new leadership style. When I began my research I didn't know I would come to the conclusion that this new leadership style would blend the best of the male and female. I just knew it had to be different from the command-and-control, top-down, John Wayne, "I'm in charge and will save the day"-type of leader. As I interviewed employees across the country, common threads started to appear. I've mentioned many of these findings already. As I gained perspectives by gender, age, and background, it became clear that this new leader would need a special combination of skills. I challenged myself to think of those whom I viewed as great leaders. I continued to come back to Jesus Christ. My faith has always played a big role in my life, and I came to the conclusion that Jesus Christ offers a brilliant leadership example. Who else do you know who can take murderers and make them saints? "But Jesus Christ was perfect," you say, "and we are not." You are right, but even by just striving to emulate some of his behaviors, I believe that we will be much better off than we are now.

Things have become better in the twenty-first century already due to dramatic workforce changes. One of my clients, Paula, recently went through a transition from one company to another because she decided she wanted to join a new company that was more open to meeting her nontraditional needs. When she reached the final negotiation stages of starting the relationship with her new employer, she hit a snag. Her new employer is nearly two thousand miles from where she currently lives. When the new company asked Paula about agreeing to a start date thirty days from the final agreement, she replied that that she couldn't accept after all, that the time frame and the distance of the company just wouldn't work for her life responsibilities.

The company asked her what she would propose as an alternative. She suggested that she would be willing to start at their designated time, but she could only agree to it if the company allowed her to spend the first two weeks in her current physical location and if they would authorize additional trips home for the weekends. She explained to her manager that she knows from experience the only way she can perform at her highest level is for her personal responsibilities to be taken care of, and that includes the well-being of her husband and children. She went on to say that by making the minor adjustments, the company would be demonstrating a willingness to accept her for what she brings to the table, family included. She took a risk and asked for what she wanted. This kind of activity will become the norm in the twenty-first century.

Paula is fired up! In exchange for her new employers demonstrating that they valued her, on her own time she conducted research about the market and the industry. She knows that it's smart business to do so, but she also has a sense of gratitude that translates into a willingness to engage at a higher, more intensive level. Because the leaders of this company were willing to meet her needs, they landed an employee who is ready to go above and beyond the call of duty. Unfortunately, this doesn't happen very often, but it should.

Most of the change that is occurring in the corporate environment is coming from fairly new companies. Companies that have long histories have been slow to recognize and adjust to the changes that are occurring in the workforce. As a result, many of them are struggling to incorporate behaviors and policies that are going to maintain the company's competitive edge. These older, established companies still have CEOs at the helm who can't relate to the needs and desires of today's workforce. Most of them are older, white men with stay-at-home wives who take care of the domestic responsibilities, leaving the men free to tend to business. The problem is that CEOs who have not been sensitized to the changing world still believe that policies and procedures that were put in place twenty years ago—such as rigid work schedules, private networks, and nepotism—still work today. They don't work today!

How does your company measure up? Have you taken the steps needed to understand the changing face and needs of today's workforce? Have you done anything about it? Have you paid lip service or truly taken action that you can measure? What would your employees say?

PART 2

THE
SOLUTION

CHAPTER 4

It's Time for a New Leadership Style

Most leaders are teachers at heart. If you have no desire to be a mentor,
you have no place being a leader

—Steve Adubato

What Employees Need and Want in a Leader

Employees want a leader they can connect with, build a relationship with, trust, respect, and so much more. Twenty-first-century employees want and deserve a leader who can foster an environment where everyone can succeed. Employees want an environment that is enjoyable. In order to be able to move the 80 percent of employees who don't want to go to work on Monday mornings to 80 percent who do, leaders need to give their people something to look forward to.

What employees don't want is a fake boss, a "do as I say but not as I do" kind of leader. Employees want to work for a leader who is real—no game faces allowed. The *Harvard Business Review* puts it this way: "When you stop pretending to be perfect, people start wanting to work with you." One of the biggest frustrations shared by many people I interviewed was their utter disgust with the number of meetings that occur in the business environment. Most of these meetings were viewed as being useless. Many said that their leader called employees together simply to hear himself pontificate. Okay, aren't we supposed to be looking for efficiencies?

Employees want a leader who has a vision, has an efficient roadmap to get there, can connect everyone to the vision and create an environment where everyone can thrive. This is part of the formula to motivate employees and to give them something to look forward to. No one wants to work for a leader who is only interested in him or herself.

A New Twist on Leadership: Introducing the Hybrid Leader

It is time to focus on a new style of leadership. This new leadership style holds the key to taking the 80 percent of unsatisfied workers and moving them to 80 percent of those who love to go work and give 100 percent every day!

This leadership style is the most provocative, progressive, and powerful insight on leadership available to date in the twenty-first century. I call the men and women who will use this new leadership style "hybrid leaders." The hybrid leader represents a balanced blend of traditional male and female leadership beliefs, values, philosophies, behaviors, and styles. This style moves beyond the masculine and feminine leadership models and passes through the androgynous leadership style to a style that recognizes and values the strengths of each gender to create a new, quite special leadership style.

There is limited if any published information that talks about the value of the female in the work environment. Perhaps the best source of information on helping people understand the value of women in the workplace is a book entitled *America's Competitive Secret: Woman Managers*. Author Dr. Judy Rosener, a professor in the Graduate School of Management at the University of California, was one of the early pioneers focusing on the ways that women and men lead. She is also the author of the celebrated *Harvard Business Review* article, "Ways Women Lead," and coauthor of *Workforce America! Managing Employee Diversity as a Vital Resource.* I had an opportunity to interview Dr. Rosener and was inspired by her courage to be bold about her belief, the same belief I share: the best leaders combine the best of the male and female leadership styles. Alice Eagly is yet another pioneer in the study of women and men in leadership positions. Eagly's article entitled "Do Women Make Better Bosses Than Men?" offered a thought-provoking argument about the many benefits of women as leaders. Not only is there an argument for integrating the strengths of the female leader, but it also reflects the changing dynamic of the consumer. Combined, minorities and women contribute more than $5.2 trillion annually to the U.S. economy (*WOW! Facts 2002*), yet the glass ceiling has been and is still real. As of 2002, women represented 12.5 percent of corporate officers in Fortune 500 companies (Catalyst). And on average, according to "Female Executives Display Business Savvy" in *USA Today*, women have to be better executives than their male counterparts.

Females in today's business environment are no longer comfortable conforming to the traditional masculine leadership model. Dr. Rosener suggests that conformity is expected because of the "one best model" theory. In other words, women must act like men to be viewed as credible. As you'll see later, even when women conform, they still don't win. Women are expected to live up to society's perceptions of the roles that women should play, and they should be able to act like men without acting too much like men. Confusing? Yes!

When I was climbing the corporate ladder, women had to conform in order to be viewed as "promotable material." But it wasn't what I wanted to do, to be honest, and the need to conform was one of the major reasons that I chose to leave corporate America and why many other women have done the same. What needs to happen is for the rules of leadership to be reinvented.

We have to give ourselves permission to believe in a new style of leadership. The hybrid leadership style doesn't negate the benefits of the traditional male leadership style; rather it extracts the best from the traditional male leadership style and then augments it to reflect a style that has far more impact in the twenty-first century. But I must be clear. I do not believe that the "traditional" style of leadership, which has been credited to the male, works in today's environment. As so correctly stated in *Fast Company* magazine's article "Your Job Is Change," in the old economy, leadership was another way of saying "formal authority." In the new economy, power comes from knowledge and creativity.

In fact, research shows that today's workforce is far more responsive to a leader who has solid business acumen (traditionally associated with men) wrapped in behavior that is collaborative and open (traditionally associated with women). The challenges we face in the work environment will not be solved by the current command-and-control type of leader. These dynamic and complex issues demand a leadership style that is much different from what we have ever known.

There are countless books on leadership. However, with 80 percent of employees not wanting to go to work on Monday and with many of them attributing this feeling primarily to the poor relationship or lack of relationship with their boss, we clearly haven't found the right leadership formula. As Marie-Therese Claes states in her article, "Women, Men and Management Styles," "The masculine and feminine models must coexist and operate in synergy."

Hybrid leaders are open, collaborative, and unafraid to show emotions. They are caring and ready to admit they don't have all the answers. Hybrid leaders will be catalysts for transformation throughout corporate America. Through this transformation these new leaders will be able to reconnect each organization's vision to its greatest asset: its people. This reconnection will result in increased productivity, better performance, and an enhancement of the organization's bottom line.

Why aren't leaders currently demonstrating these kinds of skills? Many leaders demonstrate various components of what I deem to be hybrid leader traits, but with very few exceptions do most leaders possess skills and demonstrate behavior that totally aligns with the hybrid leadership style. But there is an even deeper reason that most leaders don't display a blending of both male and female styles. To better understand, we have to go back to when we were little girls and boys. The adults that we have become today are directly tied to the lessons we learned at a very early age. It's not that our parents and grandparents wanted to teach us things that wouldn't work. They taught us ideals and philosophies based upon their world, but the world has changed. It's time to let go of the old ways of thinking, particularly about gender and leadership.

Our parents and grandparents told us things like little girls deal with stress by crying. They told little boys that boys don't cry, just suck it up and be tough. Deborah Tannen, a noted author on gender and communication topics, conducted a history study on childhood development and its impact upon adult lives. She found girls to be less confident and boys to be more confident. Why? Because little girls were told things like "Good girls don't brag." Boys, on the other hand, were taught to show their pride.

Now these little girls and boys have grown up and become adults who go to work. In the work environment, we say to the girls who are now women, "You need to market yourself to get to the top." To the boys who are now men we say, "Show some emotions so people think you care." These grown-up children look at us like we have five heads. No wonder we develop leaders who don't know how to balance being strategic with being compassionate. No wonder they don't know how to display emotional strength and prowess. No one has ever taught them how. Even though things have changed in the world, these adults who are now vice presidents, senior vice presidents, and CEOs haven't given themselves permission to change.

The truth of the matter is that little girls and boys are born wired differently, which should come as no surprise. Despite the hard-wiring differences, both genders are born with many of the same abilities. I truly believe that God designed women and men in the way that he did to compensate for each other's limitations, strengths, and weaknesses. My contention is that because of society's stereotypes, each gender suppresses many of the gifts that are the same. As a result, we hinder the ability for men and women to leverage their natural gifts to become leaders who can balance both the right and left sides of the brain. In essence, society places females and males in boxes marked with behavior that is deemed appropriate for that gender. How wrong is that? Why shouldn't it be okay for little boys to cry? When you slam your finger in the door, it hurts regardless of your gender.

I have a plea to make to parents who are reading this point, and to uncles and aunts and godparents who don't have their own children: Please stop raising children using outdated society rules about the boys and girls "should" behave. Focus instead on building character. Place extra emphasis on helping them learn how to express their authentic selves. Try to help them see that while all people are created differently, there are many commonalities that should be celebrated.

My father and mother raised ten children. They raised us with the mind-set that the girls could do exactly what the boys could do and vice versa. My mother was the disciplinarian in the home. She exemplified the essence of the top-down leadership model. Her favorite saying was that there was room for only one attitude in her house: hers. My father, on the other hand, was the peacemaker. He wanted everyone to get along. He was the encourager, a gentle but firm spirit. He wanted all of his kids to focus on several key areas: character, strong work ethic, service to others, honoring God, and continuous learning. He considered these to be the cornerstones of life.

He loved to try to fix broken things. He would say that broken things are still good; they just need a little work. He would tinker with broken things like irons or vacuum cleaners. Most of the time the things that he said were "fixed" never worked more than a couple of times after he fixed them. But he'd go right back and try to fix it again. Through this he taught us the principle of never giving up. He had always wanted to be a lawyer, but times were unkind to black men in the years that he was growing up, and that dream never came true. But to compensate for his strong desire to study law, he would read law books. He believed in teaching oneself whatever one needed to know. He and my mother balanced each other out.

Gerdiest, my mother, would beat you from the front door to the back door. She was the suck-it-up, tough-love queen, but she believed in the potential of each of her children. She didn't believe in race ever being served up as a reason for us not making it. She would say, "We've paid the price so that your generation can have the power of choice." Why do I share these stories with you? I want you to see that behavior is learned, and philosophies and beliefs are shaped by life experiences. Hard wiring is hard wiring, but the rest is learned, be it negative or positive.

Here is a good example that demonstrates the point. Both men and women experience emotion, yet if a woman cries in the work environment, she is viewed as weak. But men express their emotions in the work environment as well. The way that they often express their emotions is through cursing and raising their voices. Why do men express themselves this way? Men (and boys) have been taught to express only anger, so sadness is expressed as anger. Resentment and fear are also expressed as anger. Crying and yelling are both ways to express emotion. So why shouldn't it be okay for women to cry when they are upset?

Expressing emotion is just one of the areas where men and women are held to different standards in the work environment. This particular area of focus, emotional response, can easily become a major source of conflict, miscommunication, and frustration. Left unresolved, it can even lead to depression. Unfortunately, most people don't know when they are truly depressed, and often they don't even know why. Do you think that any of these workplace dynamics could be contributing factors? I do. When people cannot be authentic, something gets out of balance in their spirit. This imbalance is a cause of depression. How do any of us behave when we are unhappy?

Here is the bottom line according to Linda Bush, a noted

expert on BrainStyles®: We need to understand the connection between hard wiring, learned behavior, and choice. Hard wiring refers to how the left and right hemispheres of the brain are accessed at different speeds and in different sequences, performing different functions. Hard wiring is genetically determined. Hardwired decision-making sequences can be grouped into four general patterns, and these patterns determine one's BrainStyle. Based upon the BrainStyles® assessment tool combined with her experience and extensive research, Linda asserts that when you understand your BrainStyle, you can better exercise your power of choice. You know when to pause to allow yourself time to process, either by yourself or with someone else, in an effort to come to the best answer, a more complete solution. But you must be willing to embrace new data that is introduced and be willing to translate it into behavior.

In an extended interview on this topic, Linda validated a belief that I had been pondering for some time: we shouldn't focus on trying to "change" people. Rather we should focus on leveraging what she refers to as "time zero." Time zero is the authentic yet vulnerable moment when there is no reference point for the decision maker to pull from for help. In other words, time zero is the moment when we make a decision based not on experience or analysis but instead on instinct. At the moment of time zero, each of us can

- Leverage our hard wiring (knowledge of your BrainStyle helps you recognize your hardwired responses).

- Manage the way we process data through the hard-wiring baseline.

- Pause so that we don't automatically default to behavior that has been acquired through stereotypes, but instead make an intentional choice about implementing new behavior based upon processing both old data and new data.

I'm not asking you to erase what you've learned in life. Instead, what I'm inviting you to do is to give yourself permission to accept the new philosophies that will make you a leader who can connect with and harness the greatest characteristics of today's workforce. I know that many of you may already be thinking this is too "soft" for you. To those of you who are thinking this, please hang in there with me. Maybe I can help you begin to believe just a little bit more.

Let me offer another practical understanding of how our learned behavior or "programming" affects and shapes who we are. Shad Helmstetter, Ph.D., a leading behavioral psychologist and authority in the field of self-management and author of the book, *What to Say When You Talk to Yourself*, makes several key points to support the assertion that beyond hard wiring we are the products of learned behavior:

- Programming creates beliefs.

- Beliefs create attitudes.

- Attitudes create feelings.

- Feelings determine actions.

- Actions create results.

Helmstetter asserts that the way to overcome negative programming is to engage in self-talk. Through self-talk anyone who has the desire can begin to reshape thoughts and, ultimately, behavior.

Somewhere in our programming we have formed an idea of what a great leader looks like. The image that most of us have been programmed to accept is likely composed of one, if not all, of the following attributes: male, militaristic, top-down, got all the answers . . . you get the image. According to the *Harvard Business Review* article "It's Hard Being Soft," in the *Best of HBR on Leadership*, "The stereotypical leader is a solitary tough guy, never in doubt and immune to criticism. Real leaders break that mold. They invite candid feedback and even admit they don't have all the answers." Now how can you argue with one of the world's most renowned authorities on leadership?

The truth is that there is still a double standard for men

and women regarding leadership. In fact, one of my clients put it this way: "When you are a woman and you have babies, then you are no longer considered 'promotable.' But if you are a man and your wife has babies, then you are 'committed and settling down.'" When I was in corporate just a few years ago, these were the stereotypes and struggles I saw for women and men:

- When men were seen talking at the water cooler, they were viewed as strategizing. When women were seen talking at the water cooler, they were wasting time and gossiping.

- When men asked for the next promotion, they were seen as "aggressive and dedicated." When women asked for the next promotion, they were seen as "too ambitious" or overstepping their boundaries.

- When a man spent a lot of time with a fellow male colleague or boss, it was viewed as "male bonding" and "networking." When a woman spent time with a male counterpart, they were suspected of having an affair.

- When a woman left the office early, she was viewed as not being able to balance her family and professional responsibilities. If a man left the office early, they'd say, "He must have an appointment with a client."

- When women got together for a group lunch, they were viewed as acting like "high-schoolers." When men got together in a group for lunch, they were viewed as keeping the "good ol' boy" club going.

We need to get beyond these stereotypes. We cannot achieve the kind of breakthrough results that we desire without finding a way to overcome them.

But it can be done. Accept my invitation to be a leader who can:

- Be authentic

- Show that you care

- Be open

- Put people first

- Have fun in the work environment

- Show emotions in the workplace

- Refine "power" to mean "service to others"

- Achieve great results by developing great people

Why do you want to accept this invitation? The answer is simple: You will be more successful as a leader than you could have ever imagined. If you truly want to be a leader who can be a catalyst for greatness, I urge you to take to heart the message that I offer about the value of becoming a hybrid leader.

We need leaders who aren't power hungry but hungry to empower! We need leaders who can challenge the status quo instead of becoming yes men or women. We need leaders who value the power of emotions. We need leaders who believe in collaboration. We need leaders who are interested not only in the end result but in how the results are achieved.

We've got to restore the core of leadership, which is service to others. You know what will happen as a result of becoming this kind of leader? People who work for you will want to come to work. They will go that extra mile. They will begin thinking creatively so that they can innovate and find new approaches to the business. They will become more committed.

"But why?" you may ask. Because they will feel like they belong. By acknowledging the contribution to the success of the organization that each and every employee has, you actually unlock the vault of loyalty and commitment that prompts employees to want to give the highest possible level of contribution. It's absolutely amazing what happens when employees know that their leader cares.

I have coached many developing leaders in my twenty-two years of business. During the last three years as a business/ executive coach I consistently found that the problems most developing leaders face are not related to their technological skills; it's in their ability to connect with their team.

Perhaps you are sitting there saying, "Well, I'm not in charge at work, so what can I do with this information? I'm not a leader, I'm a follower." To which I say: You are a leader. You know where leadership starts? It starts with you. It is not about a title; it is about behavior that serves as the catalyst for corporate transformation.

Mahatma Gandhi said, "You've got to become the change you want to see in the world," which means you've got to get into the game, no matter what your position is in the company. Instead of focusing on why the company is outsourcing yet another department, come up with a new approach to the business. Instead of allowing the stress to eat at you and rob you of energy, do something about it. Accept personal responsibility for yourself!

If you are thinking that this type of leader doesn't exist, I say that you are both right and wrong. Pieces exist. I encourage you to take on a new position of leadership. It will take courage to lead the needed transformation, but anyone is capable of doing it. Get into the game. Stop waiting for the boss, your mother, or your colleague to do it. You can do this. You can be a part of changing the work environment. You can start this transformation in yourself and in your company!

Hybrid Leader Anchors and Tenets

It will take strong leadership to regain a level of employee commitment and loyalty that will translate into higher levels of productivity. It will take compassion, dedication, and courage to change the outdated management style that worked for a few into one that works for every employee. The hybrid leader will be the key to reconnecting employees and creating breakthrough results. The rest of this chapter presents a way to gain a deep understanding of the behaviors of this leader. I encourage you to go to the Web site www.workforexcellence.com to take the hybrid leader assessment before you continue this chapter. Completing this assessment will provide you with a backdrop to evaluate your current leadership behaviors. After you have completed the assessment, you'll be able to better target the areas that you must address in order to become a hybrid leader yourself.

Leadership: Men and Women

Let's examine more closely the leadership style differences between men and women. My observations in this area are rooted in years of research and also from my own corporate experience. First, let me set the record straight. There are, of course, both men and women who possess combinations of these behaviors, values, beliefs, and competencies. This review is very general in scope and should therefore be taken in that context.

The following chart outlines general male and female leadership behaviors. I want to encourage you to challenge yourself to see how many of the behaviors are incorporated into your current leadership style. Remember, all of them have good and bad points. The successful people are those who sharpen the good points and neutralize the bad points.

MALE	FEMALE
Independent	Dependent
Resistant to change	Resistant to change
Wants to be supportive but may not know how to express it	Supportive, sometimes to a flaw
Competitive	Collaborative
Egotistical	Caring
Thinks hierarchically	Thinks even playing field
Self-confident	Underdeveloped confidence

continued

Decisive	Intuitive
Direct communicator	Direct but sensitive communicator
Aggressive	Assertive
Emotional avoidance	Emotional intention
Results-oriented	Results-oriented
MALE	**FEMALE**
People-focused to a point	People-focused from the core
Limited flexibility	Flexible
Strategic thinker	Less developed strategic thinking ability
Strong technical skills	Quickly advancing in the technical area
Controlling	Empowerment
Family men with minimal household responsibilities	Strong sensitivities toward understanding work/life balance issues
Holds information	Shares information
Tells people what to do	Teaches people how to do a task
Slow to give credit to others openly	Openly acknowledges others
Good at making tough decisions	Sometimes afraid to make a decision that will disappoint others

What's interesting is that when a woman displays very many of the behaviors that are generally viewed as being "masculine," she is viewed as a "B," which doesn't stand for bad, bold, or beautiful. Now let's take a look at how these behaviors, beliefs, and values drive the way men and women perform in the work environment.

Men and Women in the Workplace

"Women in management tend to have a more relationship oriented style of leadership than men, one that emphasizes supporting and developing their employees," according to Eagly and Johnson in "Gender and Leadership Styles: A Meta-Analysis." To further analyze the difference between how men and women act and react both in and out of the workplace, review the following list adapted from the work of Dr. Marianne Legato, M.D., founder and director of gender-based medicine, Columbia University.

KEY AREAS OF FOCUS

✓ Thinking Process

Men

- More linear and factual
- Geared to think more sexually
- Choices made based upon outward appearances

Women

- More conceptual
- Intuitive
- Embrace a broad and collaborative process
- Challenged by the ability to separate personal feelings from the task at hand
- Thinking linked to some emotion and the essence of who is involved

✓ Negotiations

Men

- Initiate negotiations about four times as often as women
- Describe negotiations as "winning a ball game" or a "wrestling match"

Women

- Have a great deal of apprehension about negotiations
- Describe the negotiation process as "going to the dentist"
- Typically ask for less when they negotiate
- Seek a win/win so that everyone can be happy

✓ Communications

Men

- Skewed towards speaking directly and telling people what to do
- More likely to interrupt others
- Frequently repeat ideas that have already been shared and then position the idea as their own
- Less eye contact

Women

- More likely to allow interruptions without stopping the interrupters
- Tend to make statements that sound like a question

✓ Conflict

Men

- Very comfortable with taking a hard-line position
- Like to "one-up" the other party

Women

- Want to get the conflict over so that people can be happy

✓ Business Relationships

Men

- Assumed relationship
- Common ground is achieved simply because of gender
- Find it very easy to work with people they don't like

Women

- There is no assumed relationship
- Chit-chat as a way of connection
- Haven't learned in totality how to support other women
- Find working with people that they don't like very difficult because everything is about an emotional connection

✓ Power

Men

- Link power to authority
- Find it very easy to employ power associated with title
- Power motivates greater achievement

Women

- Linked to service
- Give orders using soft language (asking rather than telling)
- Feel everyone is equal, no matter who has the position of authority

✓ Decision Making/Problem Solving

Men

- Focused on getting the problem solved quickly so that they can move onto the next item

Women

- More concerned about how problems are solved than the solving of the problem itself

✓ Emotions and Bad Experiences

Men

- Want to get alone by themselves and think in private
- Express emotions by using a loud voice, cursing
- Recall events based upon numbers, strategies, or activities

Women

- Want to tell their story to everyone
- Want others to understand what they've gone through
- Express emotions through faster speaking, higher voice tones, hand movement
- Easily recall memories that are connected to emotions

✓ Stress Relief

Men

- Golf
- Drinks
- Fantasy play (video games, fantasy sports, etc.)
- Vegetating in front of the television

Women

- Shopping
- Talking
- Crying
- Exercising

✓ Gathering Information

Men

- Don't like to ask questions, as they want to appear as though they already know the answer

Women

- Ask lots of questions as a way of showing interest and connecting

✓ Workplace Values

Men

- Pay
- Benefits
- Achievement
- Success

- Authority

Women

- Friends at work

- Recognition

- Respect

- Communication

- Collaboration

For a great deal of the leaders who currently sit at all levels of management, the male behaviors and values apply. The degree to which you can swing between these descriptions, or incorporate both of them, depends upon how you were raised. I have observed, however, that male leaders from Generations X and Y tend to incorporate more of the traditionally viewed female behaviors and values. Even some male baby boomers have adopted certain behaviors that are traditionally considered feminine. Men are starting to understand and value all of their responsibilities in a more holistic way. Men still recognize the importance of professional achievements, but they are no longer willing to fulfill their career dreams at the price of a personal life.

How do you stack up against these tendencies? Are you currently a leader who knows the difference between "telling" and "teaching" someone how to do a task? Do you shy away from making tough decisions? Do you believe that it is okay to show your emotions in the workplace? Or do you put your game face on each morning so that no one gets to know the real you? What do you think would happen if we combined these tendencies? What kind of a leader would have these traits? The hybrid leader!

Hybrid leaders are committed to developing teams where they swim together or sink together. They are the new breed of leaders who have the courage and commitment to make positive and needed organizational change in order to optimize the twenty-first-century workforce. These leaders possess a core value of respect for people as the company's greatest asset. This new breed is committed to aligning human resources to the organization's strategy, thus enabling breakthrough results and a positive impact on productivity and the bottom line. Hybrid leaders lead based upon principles that they hold to be cornerstones drawn from male and female beliefs and behaviors. The following list forms the essence of their leadership platform.

- Valuing each employee as a "whole" person
- True empowerment with accountability
- Cross-functional collaboration
- Willingness to honor nontraditional workforce needs
- Inclusion
- Celebration, not tolerance, of the unique and differing contributions made by each employee
- Transparent communications
- Service to others
- Humility
- Embracing change as an opportunity
- Assuming personal responsibility for the success of his or her people
- Giving people a reason to follow
- Opening to and following up on feedback

Hybrid leaders must commit to engaging in every facet of the business—and not only engaging, but learning and sharing information that can support new ways of building the business and increasing profitability.

The next section of the chapter focuses on a couple of key areas that I believe represent the greatest immediate opportunities. In the last part of this book, I present some mini case studies of the way a hybrid leader would handle additional important areas of leadership responsibility.

Motivating the Team

I have read so many leadership books that suggest that it is not the leader's responsibility to motivate his or her people because people should motivate themselves. I do agree that people need to be able to motivate themselves, but I also believe that the leader's responsibility is to inspire and to serve as motivation for his or her people. Motivation is an underlying connection to the core of gaining emotional buy-in. In a time when employees are full of pain and companies are looking for new ways to advance the business, why wouldn't it be a leader's responsibility to motivate his or her people to achieve better results? Everyone in the organization needs to recognize the importance of developing new ways to motivate employees.

I'm not suggesting that every team needs to have the weekly "big blue Wal-Mart rally," although if it works, do it. What I am suggesting is that motivation is as critical a component of getting great results as laying out a brilliant plan. Honestly, when you think about it, motivating others isn't that difficult. Sometimes just a simple thank-you can do the trick, or giving credit where credit is due, or being considerate when an employee is facing difficulty. These kinds of things motivate people. It's not always money. If you truly don't know where to begin, try asking each of your employees what motivates him or her. You'll be surprised at the answers you get.

Hybrid leaders serve as motivators by creating environments where people can thrive. They also recognize that helping others realize their own significance opens the door for great things to occur. When leaders offer motivating experiences for their employees, they are creating more capacity for higher levels of contribution. When people have a sense of being important, you can expect great things to happen. It also reinforces the focus on team contribution.

Hybrid leaders serve as role models to encourage a culture that mirrors their own philosophies. They sow deep seeds that support small wins, guiding the transformation to reshape and position a company where each and every employee lives by the

HYBRID LEADERSHIP PRINCIPLES

- We embrace and celebrate the power of differences.
- We focus on providing innovative, quality products for our consumers.
- We win together or lose together.
- We leave politics to politicians.
- We communicate with total transparency.
- We value empowerment with accountability.
- We constantly look for new ways to learn from each other.
- We reject bureaucracy.
- We develop strong leaders who can serve others.
- We strive to demonstrate our commitment to work/ life balance.
- We seek breakthrough results through constant innovation.
- We believe that work should be fun.

following tenets, rather than just reading them on the wall and forgetting them:

How many of you could stop right now and repeat the tenets that drive your company's culture? How many of you would then be able to say that the employees live by those tenets?

Google, the world's largest search engine organization, was featured on 60 *Minutes* because of the success that the company has experienced despite the downturn in the dot-com industry. Google lives by many of the tenets listed above. I was particularly struck by the fact that not only are people valued, they are encouraged to have fun. Encouraged? Yes, encouraged. In fact, they see laughter, parties, and excitement as key ingredients for creativity and innovation. As Eric Schmit, Google's forty-nine-year-old CEO, put it, "It is important to feel good about where you work. The tenet of 'do no evil' is the code that drives our business conduct day in and day out." Some of the other tenets that Google's culture is built on include: Innovation is the company's bloodline; appreciation is the best motivation; work and play are not mutually exclusive; we love our employees, and we want them to know it.

I can remember once being in a meeting with my colleagues where someone made a statement that caused the room to erupt in laughter. My boss was not present when this occurred, but a moment later he walked in and said, "Hey, there is way too much fun going on in here. Let's get back to work." That's the way it is in many companies today. People walk around like they've got ramrods strapped to their backs because they think someone else thinks it makes them look like a leader.

The energy that comes from working in an environment where you can sing, laugh out loud, play games, and talk at the water cooler is incredibly positive. Do you know how many of the world's problems have been solved at the water cooler? Lots. But so many people are afraid that if they are seen at the cooler they will lose their job because it looks like they don't have anything else to do but talk. Okay, don't you have to talk to solve problems? Isn't that what problem solving is all about? Brainstorming and talking it through?

Bringing the aforementioned tenets alive is what the hybrid leader strives for day in and day out. Once these tenets become a permanent part of your daily activities, you will connect with your employees in a way that touches their hearts. There you will find the treasure for an emotional bond that will be the source of restoring levels of commitment, energy, and excitement that will translate into meaningful results. These tenets become the filters through which everything that this leader does is screened. Once again, you are probably thinking this is a dream. It's not a dream. Creating this leadership style is a must. It is an imperative for success in the twenty-first century. It may be scary, different, and challenging, but boy, is it ever worth it.

The Root System of a Hybrid Leader

If your actions inspire others to dream more, learn more, do more,
and become more, you are a leader.

—John Quincy Adams

I wanted to really sharpen my ability to serve as a business/executive coach, so I began interviewing everyone I could, asking all kinds of questions about the challenges and opportunities that people face in today's work environment. I wanted to make sure that I first clearly understood the problem so that I could determine what kind of leadership style would be needed to address the problems. After interviewing hundreds of managers and leaders at every level within numerous organizations, I came to an interesting conclusion. There are leadership behaviors that male leaders have and leadership behaviors that female leaders have, and each thinks his or her way is the right way. I would humbly submit that both genders are wrong. What I'm proposing is a new way.

The leader who will experience the greatest success going forward will be the leader who can combine the best of male leadership behavior and values with the best of female leadership behavior and values.

As this is a new concept in leadership, let me slow down and do the deep dive so that you see what I see. The first question that you might have is this one: What does a hybrid leader look like? Hybrid leaders look like the men and women who go to work every day. The potential for this new leader can be found in every culture, every race, and both genders. The hybrid leader knows himself or herself and understands the desire for leadership. He or she has a personal vision and takes full ownership for bringing that vision to fruition. Many leaders think they know themselves, but, truth be told, they don't. Management consultant Warren G. Bennis, author of several books on leadership, says, "If knowing yourself and being yourself were as easy to do as to talk about, there wouldn't be nearly so many people walking around in borrowed postures, spouting second-hand ideas, trying desperately to fit in rather than to stand out." The hybrid leader is not afraid to take the road less traveled. He or she has conviction and therefore is willing to take stands that others may consider unpopular.

Let's take the time to flesh out this matrix. These definitions are prescribed by the hybrid leader belief system.

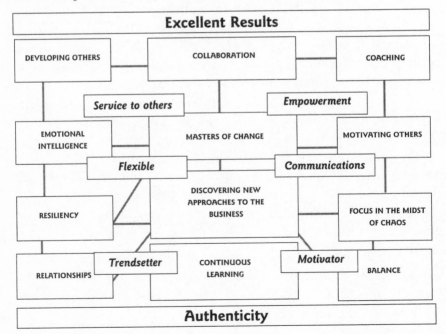

The Hybrid Leader Competency Matrix

As we peel back the onion to look at the competencies of a hybrid leader, I encourage you to spend some time evaluating your own abilities in these key areas. Capture your own thoughts that you come up with as there is room for your own perspective.

What does it mean to be authentic as a leader?

- Knowing your own core values
- Displaying consistent behavior
- Recognizing that there is nothing called "perfection"
- Honoring a sense of purpose

How does a hybrid leader mentor, coach, and motivate or inspire his or her people?

- Connects with others at the emotional level
- Subscribes to a belief that people are the company's greatest asset
- Values and celebrates differences for the wealth of innovation and creativity that they offer
- Ties empowerment to accountability
- Demonstrates a commitment to development of others
- Adheres to a service mentality

What enables the hybrid leader to be an effective communicator?

- Uses every language (not just technical jargon to make him- or herself feel good)

- Openly embraces feedback and takes action
- Believes in being transparent
- Believes listening is the most important part of communication

What makes a hybrid leader a trendsetter?

- Embracing change as an opportunity
- Possessing a desire to create the future
- Being a student of the world
- Recognizing that innovation is the key to sustained success

Why do people want to follow a hybrid leader?

- The level of dedication to excellence
- The commitment to honor employees holistically
- The commitment to continuous learning
- The authentic and real way a hybrid leader acts
- The admission that the leader doesn't have all the answers
- The lack of reluctance to challenge the status quo
- The assumption of personal responsibility

How does a hybrid leader get breakthrough results?

- Builds great relationships
- Draws on resiliency
- Forgives and forgets negative experiences

- Keeps eyes focused on the prize
- Collaborates with others who can help to advance ideas
- Knows how to share success

How can this leader be that good? Discipline, dedication, and determination. Hybrid leaders are not perfect, and they know it, so they are always in a state of self-examination and growth.

The Blending Comes Alive

In an interview with a male vice president from Verizon Wireless in Dallas, Texas, we talked about the trend toward men openly displaying a commitment to their parental responsibilities. This man is an awesome leader. He and his team are consistently rewarded for providing outstanding customer service internally and externally. He shared a story with me about a meeting that was to be held on the same day that his daughter was having Princess Day. He called the host of the meeting and shared that he could not attend because of the promise that he had made to his daughter to be with her. Years ago a male leader might have called and cancelled his participation in a meeting, but I bet it wouldn't be because of parental responsibilities, or at least he wouldn't have admitted it. He would probably say something such as, "I have a meeting conflict that I just can't resolve." The fact that this man was bold enough to be open with the importance of serving as a father is great!

Many leaders recognize the need for change, except when it comes to their own leadership style. Based upon my interviews, more men than women seem to think that a leader has to be skewed toward all male behaviors with no exceptions. That is absolutely wrong. The women I interviewed saw some male behaviors that they thought were of importance in becoming a good leader, but these women didn't understand how to leverage their natural feminine traits. Specific masculine behaviors such as being decisive and keeping calm under intense pressure were cited as positive by the women I interviewed. In general, men address problems clearly while women can be more passive/ aggressive, especially with problems concerning other people.

Warren G. Bennis stated in 1997 that the competitive advantage would be gained from the leadership of women. He argued that feminine traits contain the potential for improving the human condition and that society must dispel the myth that the only way for women managers to survive is to act like men. The irony is that male leaders have been trying to shed the same macho character traits that women have been encouraged to imitate.

Senior leaders will have to get to a point where they are able to see the benefits of this new leadership style. It is of the highest level of importance to see what kind of leadership style develops as a result of combining the best of both genders.

A Closer Look at Your Own Personal Belief System

There are many different leadership styles. You have developed your own style. You've learned by drawing on others. Your leadership style is built on your experiences and philosophies or beliefs. These beliefs guide the manner in which you are able to connect with people of all backgrounds, adjust your communication style, serve others, embrace flexibility, pursue innovation with vigor, and achieve breakthrough results. At the risk of sounding redundant, as the world changes, leaders must change. Leaders must challenge themselves to examine their own limited perceptions of people who approach the business differently, possess different values, and have different professional expectations. A guided self-discovery of deep-seated beliefs is the foundation upon which awareness and behavioral changes can be made.

Despite the fact that leadership has been a topic of focus for decades, a shortage of quality leaders in the business environment exists even today. Why? Perhaps because people move into leadership positions without fully understanding what is required of a leader. Perhaps because people don't understand the awesome responsibility of becoming a leader. Leadership is not for the faint of heart. It takes hard work, commitment, and extraordinary resilience.

Make no mistake about it: leadership begins with yourself. You must first understand why you want to be a leader before you can become a good leader. Gaining this insight and understanding requires a deep analysis of your individual strengths and weaknesses. It also requires a deeper appreciation for your beliefs and philosophies about the list of items below. If someone were to ask you how you felt about these things, what would you say? Have you ever slowed down long enough to think about it? If not, now is as good a time as any.

Risk	Openness
Learning	Change
Motivation	Communication
Problems	People
Service	Intuition
Diversity (now Inclusion)	Integrity
Fear	Ethics
Collaboration	Future
Failure	Past
Results	Service
Mistakes	Success
Money	Death
Pain	Friends
Family	Ego

Every leader should have guiding principles that they have developed, own, and are committed to. One of the key steps I take with all of my coaching clients is to help them determine where they stand on these critical issues.

A Hybrid Leader's Personal Business Principles

Strong business principles are needed to succeed in the new frontier. As a leader in the twenty-first century, you need to lead based upon a predetermined set of principles. These principles guide your commitment to make the changes necessary to experience success, and these principles are the backbone of your ability to adapt to the hybrid leadership style.

The hybrid leader's personal operating standard is based on integrity. The hybrid leader strives to do that which is right in every facet of their personal and professional life. For example, a hybrid leader's principles might include: "I will conduct myself with the best interest of others at heart. I will prepare to make successful presentations that will include cutting-edge research, internal and external interviews to support the proposal, and pre-selling activities. I will stay on top of consumer and business trends. I will strive to introduce at least one new best practice based upon proven application to the organization at large." The core competencies of the hybrid leader that we previously examined offer tremendous insight into the principles that guide the hybrid leadership style. I'm only going to spend time on the one or two things that weren't called out previously. I'd like to focus on helping you to develop your own principles and then challenge you to compare them to the hybrid leadership principles.

Ethical Behavior

The one area I want to make sure to cover as a critical principle is ethical behavior. Our choices as based on our beliefs form our character. I have seen people who were consistent number-one performers who had a brief lapse of judgment and became involved in unethical behavior and eventually were fired. As a hybrid leader, you must be committed to conducting yourself based upon the highest degree of integrity 100 percent of the time. There is zero tolerance in this area. Now, I'm not talking about little bitty mistakes caused as a result of poor judgment; I'm talking about significant decisions that don't align with being a leader rooted in integrity. Even one slipup is enough to make people question your credibility. Always take the high road. Don't let yourself get sucked into activities that do not align with your values and beliefs.

Resist the temptation to adopt bad practices just because it is acceptable behavior for some, even if that "some" are among the chosen in your organization. Get out, but don't compromise; once you do, you will be on the other side. Remember when you were a kid and your mom used to say that you have to tell a thousand lies to cover up for the first lie? That's what happens when you begin to engage in practices that are unethical. Don't do it!

I want to offer you one last word of caution in the area of ethical behavior, a caution that applies to all leaders regardless of gender: don't get so caught up in chasing the carrot that you allow yourself to become blinded and engage in activities that are absolutely not becoming of a true leader. Temptation is everywhere, and the business world is certainly no exception. Whether it's the temptation to borrow someone else's ideas or the temptation to cook the books, what's wrong is wrong and the severity of the outcome doesn't matter. What does matter is that leaders do what is right. Make honesty and integrity the core that supports everything you do.

Keep your focus on getting results that count and on building the kind of diverse team that will keep you performing at the highest level possible. I strongly suggest that you concentrate on developing a principle attached to how you get the desired results. This principle will become your foundation for achieving consistently high results. I know that you'll find enormous benefits from spending time to fine tune your own guiding principles. I suggest this practice to every client I coach. Many have told me that by thinking about these principles, writing them down, and then taking the time to evaluate their behavior against the principles, they experience a dramatic improvement in their daily performance. Your principles should be solid and not fluid. If you take the time to think this exercise all the way through, you should never have to change your principles, although as you grow and develop you may find that your experiences cause you to add new ones.

At a conference where I was speaking, a woman came up to me afterward and asked me about formulating guiding principles. She said to me that at one time she was solid in her beliefs but that she was afraid that she had taken ownership of her bosses' beliefs, which didn't align with her own principles. I think many people find themselves in this position. They want to remain true to the things that they believe in, but they also want to be viewed by the organizations they work for as individuals to be invested in and trusted. People are afraid if they don't agree with the status quo, they won't get very far. As we have seen in previous chapters, most of the time this is the case. My hope is that the more people find the courage to be authentic in the workplace, the easier it will be to challenge the status quo without fear!

Stop now and think about your own personal business principles. What is going to guide your continuous improvement and excellent performance? How will you stay in front of the curve? Decide now to commit yourself to continually living by your self-determined business principles. Let these principles be your compass. Let these principles be rooted in things that should change the culture of your company, such as respecting others, embracing differences, and leading by example.

If you took the time to complete the hybrid leader assessment, then you know where you stand on a lot of important components of becoming this kind of leader. Now, what do you want to do about it?

CHAPTER 5

The Hybrid Leader at Work

You don't make progress by standing on the sidelines, whimpering and complaining. You make progress by implementing ideas.

—Shirley Chisholm

Focusing on the Core

By embracing a leadership style that draws on the best of male and female behaviors and values, hybrid leaders develop a leadership style that is capable of connecting with the workforce of the new millennium. Of great importance to a hybrid leader is building relationships with and being a source of promoting relationships between other people. From knowing oneself and one's own strengths and weaknesses, to creating a relationship with each employee, to being a catalyst for change for the entire organization, the hybrid leader is determined to bring out the best in everyone. This practice brings the highest rewards both for the employees and for the organization as a whole. I wonder how many leaders are really committed to the responsibility of bringing out the best in others.

I can't tell you how many times I have heard colleagues and clients talk about inheriting employees who are underdeveloped. We all have said it. But the reality is that our responsibility as leaders is to help others develop. The employee's responsibility is to have a willingness to learn and grow. That's the deal, like it or not. So we shouldn't be complaining about developing others; we should be looking at it as an opportunity to serve.

Don't get me wrong. There comes a time when you have more than invested and the employee still doesn't come around. That's when you, as the leader, need to help him or her not just out of your department but out of the company. Making these kinds of tough decisions is a part of your role as a leader too, but only after you have honored your responsibility for exhausting every available option to develop the employee.

In order to make the impact hybrid leaders are capable of, they must know themselves thoroughly and must be absolutely dedicated to developing and implementing changes that harness the greatest of the workforce and connect employees to the company vision. Self-awareness is always the first step. How will the hybrid leader demonstrate behavior that will send a message to the team, the organization, and the world of the different kind of leadership? The hybrid leader must focus on three critical areas: personal responsibilities, team responsibilities, and organizational responsibilities.

A hybrid leader is responsible to him- or herself for:

- Honoring core values

- Walking the talk

- Remaining true to leadership principles

- Being flexible and embracing change

- Having and using emotional discipline as well as emotional intelligence

- Acquiring knowledge on a continuous basis

- Analyzing trends and implementing personal and professional strategic planning

- Committing to transparent communications so that people understand what is going on with the business at all times

Do as I Do

There is little tolerance for a leader who is good at the talk but not the walk. Employees are fed up with empty-suit leaders. They are also fed up with bureaucracy designed to do nothing more than feed personal agendas. This is why formulating personal leadership principles is so important. Without them, you can be easily swayed. The heart of the hybrid leader is focused on doing what is right. Proverbs 4:23 indicates that your heart determines why you say the things you do, why you feel the way you do, and why you act the way you do. The hybrid leader puts his behaviors to the test by asking the question: does my behavior reflect that which is right?

Have you ever noticed how some leaders can be adamantly opposed to an idea when a colleague introduces it, but when the boss endorses it they think it's the best thing since sliced bread? You know what I mean. You've probably seen this happen hundreds of times. This leader is not walking the talk.

The hybrid leader is careful to think through a position on an issue before formulating a final opinion. Once engaged in this process, the hybrid leader's viewpoint changes only if credible information is introduced which she had not taken into consideration during the analysis process, not because a new player enters the scene—and definitely not because the new player might have a position of power or a title. In fact, the hybrid leader would look at those who might display this kind of behavior as being false and weak.

Going with the Flow

Hybrid leaders are flexible, which enables them to view change as an opportunity. They believe that change is necessary to survive and thrive. In fact, they see change as the birthright to continued success. Usually when I make these kinds of statements about change, people look at me as if I just fell from the stars. "Who in the world likes change?" is the message that their body language sends. I say anyone who likes living likes change. Each and every one of us has been changing every minute since the day we were born, and if we truly want to succeed in the future, we have to move from just managing change to thriving on it.

Emotional Discipline

Daniel Goleman's book *Emotional Intelligence* did a lot to bring attention to the importance of leaders being able to draw on their emotional intuition to connect with and influence others. The number-one skill missing from most emerging leaders is emotional intelligence. It is without question that critical skills such as analytical ability, fact-based decision making, and financial acumen are vitally important. But in today's high-pressure business environment, where building authentic relationships paves the way for increased productivity, soft skills are equally important. Anyone can be taught to read a financial report; it doesn't require significant behavior change. Anyone can be taught to analyze data whether or not they are data gurus, but you can't teach beliefs. Beliefs are about choices. Learning to embrace differences and new trends requires attitude and behavior changes. These are the anchors that enhance the hybrid leader's ability to apply emotional discipline. That's why it is so important to have a deep understanding of who you are as a person.

Strategic Planning

Hybrid leaders rely on strategic analysis but aren't afraid to use intuition as a key driver. It's interesting to note that strategic planning has always been thought of as a way that a company separates itself from the competition. Strategic planning in my former industry (tobacco) was funny. Who couldn't figure out that the strategic plan would be product discounting and more discounting?

The reality is that strategic planning has to support financial planning efforts. I recently heard a thought-provoking twist on the notion of strategic thinking that perfectly aligns with the core of the hybrid leader. It was a perspective offered by Dan Burrus in an interview conducted by Marcia Steele on a CD entitled *Executive Women Power Track*. Dan Burrus says that strategic planning is financial planning in disguise. Financial focus is only one part of strategic planning. The most important part of strategic planning is creating a point of difference that can give you a competitive advantage. He goes on to say that to become good at strategic planning, you must be great at "strategic thinking."

Given that the hybrid leader is committed to creating his or her own future and the future of the organization, strategic planning is a must-have strength. Ask yourself what you see for yourself in five or ten years. In fact, I ask many of my clients to determine their endgame. When this career ends, what do you want to be capable of doing? Hybrid leaders know that you must balance current fads with future opportunities. In this same interview, Burrus talks about two kinds of trends: soft trends and hard trends. He says that hard trends are factual, visible, and predictable. One of the examples he gives is that there are 80 million baby boomers who have the majority of the money in the United States, which is also true for other industrialized nations. Looking at this trend, what will be the impact of how this age group handles its finances? As they get older, they will become more conservative in their investments. This will have an enormous influence upon the financial status of the world. This trend is so hard and predictable that its breadth and depth must be addressed. The hybrid leader will not only deal with hard trends such as these but leverage them for a competitive advantage. A leader must be able to understand the difference between a soft, or passing, trend and a hard trend. Then he or she must strategically plan so that action can be implemented for outstanding results. What's the key point according to Burrus? Pay attention! Hybrid leaders are students of the world. They study trends. They look for ways to proactively turn a trend into a sustained competitive advantage.

Extreme Communication

Hybrid leaders communicate in a direct yet sensitive way. The Bible talks about wrapping communication in a spirit of love. Wouldn't it be great if you could take a magic pill and the words that came out of your mouth were the exact words that the person or people you were talking to needed and wanted to hear? I wish! The reality is that each of us has our own style of communicating. Some, like me, are very direct. Others like to add a lot of words to paint a beautiful picture. Some people leave you guessing as to what they are trying to say, and others say nothing at all. Whatever your style, what comes out of your mouth must be truthful and transparent.

Employees want to be kept up to speed on what is happening in the company, and they expect their leader, not the company's Web site, to be the source of that communication. Most important, as called out in the core competencies of the hybrid leader, is the ability to listen. Listening is one of the most critical skills for experiencing success in the twenty-first century. You can't understand your people, customers, trends, opportunities, or new possibilities if you cannot listen. Period.

A Leader Worthy of Followers

Leaders will remain responsible for getting results. This will never change. Anyone interested in maintaining active employment will have to bring home the bacon, fry it up in the pan, and reuse the bacon fat and everything else. How you do it is what will be different. The higher level of global competition will drive new levels of performance expectations. These expectations will only be fulfilled if the leader embraces the need to focus on people as the greatest asset of the organization. Great leaders will display strong personal values and seek new ways to demonstrate the value they have for others.

Organizations can quickly gain or lose a competitive advantage by their focus or lack of focus on their people. It is easy to forget—in the midst of intense business deals, new clients, and stockholder expectations—that developing talent is what's going to keep those business deals coming. Peter Drucker offers the following belief: "In a traditional workforce the worker serves the system; in a knowledge workforce the system must serve the worker." No cookie-cutter method can solve the business issues that today's workforce is charged with completing. People who don't feel connected and valued won't invest the energy to come up with new ideas to solve problems.

Just getting results is not enough. Hybrid leaders believe that how the results are achieved is just as important. Sustained success comes only if people can continuously and creatively contribute. Far too many leaders have pursued results at all costs. In fact, they've created the cultures that have resulted in disconnected and depressed employees. Some have even left dead bodies in the path, literally.

It became clear while I was interviewing leaders at different organizational levels that men and women both believe that loss of productivity and morale (positive or negative) is directly connected to the leader. Leaders who were not able to connect with their team by building authentic relationships were viewed as less effective. Hybrid leaders are committed to getting the buy-in from their team. They recognize that in order to garner support, they must take the time needed to formulate common ground. In this common area the vision can be agreed upon and ownership can take hold. Think about it. If someone asked you the question, "Why should I follow you?" could you answer with conviction and passion? So many leaders can't answer this question. People want to follow hybrid leaders because they are savvy, open, authentic, and totally focused on the team and not on themselves. In addition, integrity must be applied all the time, not 90 percent of the time. The minute you think that no one is looking and you take an action you wouldn't otherwise take, you set yourself up for failure.

A hybrid leader is responsible to his or her employees to

- Build relationships that make each employee feel valued
- Honor nontraditional needs
- Foster an environment where success can be experienced by anyone
- Create an atmosphere of continuous learning
- Serve them and offer empowerment paired with accountability
- Create a clear line of sight to the organization's vision
- Keep them motivated
- Develop the team to perform at maximum capacities
- Elicit the greatest contribution from every employee

Employees Are People, Too

I have observed that many senior leaders start the year with good intentions to do the things necessary to elicit great performance, but something always happens. Multiple projects, unanticipated expectations, changes in the marketplace, and other events cause a loss of focus on developing people. This loss of focus seems to foster lots of busywork but not very much productivity. However, when employees are connected and have a sense of understanding for how their work adds value to the bottom line, productivity increases. In a survey conducted by the Gallup organization, 69 percent of American workers said they had the opportunity to use their strengths less than once a week; only 15 percent said they used them every day. This only happens when the right employee is in the right job reporting to the right leader. It is an awful lot to bring together, but it must be done in order for optimization to occur.

Meet Them Where They Are

Futurist Patrick Dixon suggests that organizations must realize that all the greatest strategies in the world can't replace powerful connections with people. Moreover, leaders can't make powerful connections unless they understand and believe that people are the company's greatest asset. Assets should be treated with care—protected, developed, and celebrated. What kind of relationship do you have with your team? Better yet, answer this question: if you were cramming for a last-minute presentation on a Sunday night around 10 p.m., who on your team would come help you? The problem is that people who are really good at building powerful connections are leaving corporate America by the droves. When you look at the reasons that people are leaving, it becomes fairly obvious that there is a need for change. People are leaving because corporate America doesn't foster cultures where they feel valued, where nontraditional needs are viewed as important, where points of difference are embraced rather than merely tolerated, and because they aren't encouraged to use their gifts and talents. We all know that there is a correlation between employee commitment and productivity. What I don't think we understand is the correlation between the company's visible demonstration of respect for the whole person (via leaders) and the bottom line. In a survey conducted by Redbook Research and published in an article by ICG, a division of HR.com, 90 percent of employees surveyed reported that they would work harder for a company that is willing to help them deal with their personal problems.

Every time I make a speech, at least one person comes up to me after my presentation and expresses heartfelt disappointment in how his or her leader makes him feel. Recently, a woman burst into tears. I felt so sorry for her. She said that she felt hopeless. She told me her supervisor made her feel like a piece of old clothing. Sometimes people can be so beaten down that they feel powerless.

But great performance can be achieved when people feel good about the difference they can make for the team and for the organization. When people feel vested and valued, there is almost nothing that they won't give an organization. In order to create the kind of environment where people are motivated to be creative and productive, a leader has to understand what motivates each employee. What motivates one person doesn't mean a thing to someone else. When I was an area vice president of sales in the early 1990s, I tried to use a cookie-cutter motivational strategy. My colleagues would reward their people by taking them out to play golf. I thought, *Well, if it ain't broke, don't fix it.* So after the mid-year planning process I scheduled a round of golf for the entire team. My direct reporting team was composed of two women and six men. While everyone had a good time, I couldn't help noticing that a couple of the members didn't seem as enthusiastic as I thought they would be. Given that I hadn't done anything like this before, I thought I had really stretched myself.

Over drinks we were talking about how there never seems to be enough time. The pressures of life were squeezing time for some of the most important priorities: family and spiritual growth. Someone commented that it would be nice just to be able to go to the bathroom in private. Many of you reading this book will immediately identify with that feeling. One of my managers shared that what really motivates him was having time to spend with his young kids. He wanted to be able to pick his sons up from school from time to time. Another manager said that having a wonderfully intense massage would be a great way to renew her energy. I didn't respond then, but I listened and learned. The next quarterly meeting, instead of mandating that everyone play golf, there was a menu-driven activity. My team thanked me endlessly, and all I did was demonstrate a willingness to meet their needs. I wish I had learned this lesson years before. But you live and learn. And when you know how to do better, you do better! As a result of this experience, I began to embrace flextime and encouraged my managers to use it. What I realized is that I had been placing more emphasis on face time than I cared to admit. Recognizing my own limitations as a leader and opening myself up to listen and respond to the needs of my team was freeing. It also was the key that unlocked breakthrough performance levels. Why? Because the team was vested. When my counterparts heard of the alternate activities, they weren't too happy with me. "Now we'll all have to change," was the common response. *Yes, that's right. If it's right, make the change*, was my thought. But it is often difficult for senior executives to make adjustments who have, in their minds, earned the right to call the shots. We need leaders who are willing to be ambassadors of change, adopting new behaviors that help leaders connect with today's workforce. No matter how long you have been in the workforce, no matter what title you hold, something new can be learned every day.

Business Development, the Hybrid Leader Way

To experience greater success, leaders have to make a commitment to continuous learning. Long gone are the days when you earned a degree and you had all the knowledge you needed in life. The speed of change will continue to serve as motivation for continuous learning. Technological advances continue to open up a whole new way of life. In order to keep up, everyone has to embrace the idea of lifelong learning. Strong leaders need to seek every opportunity to leverage the intellectual power of their workforce. Leaders won't have all the answers; no one will. We will all be creating and inventing as we go. As my good friend Juanell Teague describes it, we will be in "innovative chaos."

The creation of learning centers is one way for hybrid leaders to encourage new idea development. Learning centers are onsite environments that replicate the world the consumer experiences. Nestlé Purina Pet Care has an excellent learning center, which was the brainchild of James White. This center provides marketing, sales, logistics, merchandising, and many other departments with the ability to pretest product introductions in a controlled environment. It also gives anyone who is interested a daily opportunity to look at the business from a different perspective. Employees are encouraged to visit the center, and customers are welcome to view the center as well. In fact, the center serves as a great location for collaborative and strategic evaluation of new ideas. When I was in corporate we had something we called a mock store. It truly looked like a convenience store on the inside. Every facet of a real convenience store was replicated. This mock store enabled us to improve our in-store activities, test our merchandising concepts, and develop new programs that were of benefit to the retailer, the consumer, and the company.

Continuous learning can occur in many different ways. Most teams have monthly meetings to talk strategy, progress, and challenges. These types of meetings present a golden opportunity for learning. Schedule one hour per meeting to dedicate to acquiring some new knowledge. Start a business book club for your team on a quarterly basis. There are so many ways to acquire learning. What has to happen is this: leaders must become comfortable being uncomfortable. It is the only way to successfully embrace the unknown and undiscovered.

True Service to Others

Hybrid leaders see their role as one of service to others rather than as egotistical, self-promoting dictators. They also believe in true empowerment accompanied by accountability. One of the reasons that people don't contribute more is because their leader overcompensates, thinking that he or she is the only one who can do it right. In fact, some leaders are so afraid that their personal reputation will be tarnished by the tiniest mistake that they don't delegate at all. They take everything upon themselves. Listen up: just because your employee may have a different approach to the work than you do does not make them wrong and you right.

Other leaders see their role as the "dumper," delegating absolutely every responsibility. Although while I was climbing the corporate ladder, I was grateful when people dumped work on me because it provided me an opportunity to learn, I don't support dumping. Employees are already doing more with less. Everyone has to play his or her own role, including the leader.

Serve your people by

- Getting them the right resources to do their job
- Eliminating roadblocks
- Transferring knowledge by teaching
- Becoming vested in their success
- Marketing their accomplishments
- Providing honest and candid feedback (even when it is tough)

Eliciting the Greatest Contribution

One of the major responsibilities of a leader is to obtain full engagement from every employee, which is easier said than done. But there is a way. It starts with ensuring that all employees understand how their jobs contribute to the advancement of the company's vision and the bottom line. Everyone has to feel valuable, which means that the hybrid leader must make the vision clear. Moreover, the vision has to become personally owned by each employee. I was recently speaking at a company that is embarking upon a repositioning. The initiative is now two years old. In an audience of three hundred people, I asked who could articulate the company's vision. Two people out of the entire audience could verbally share the company's vision. Then I asked, "How does your role advance the company's vision?" No one answered. I was truly shocked. Take the challenge: ask every member of your team to articulate the company vision and their relationship to the vision. If you don't have 100 percent buy-in, you will never be able to elicit the greatest contribution. Never!

The second step to achieving maximum performance levels is to keep your people motivated. When I was in corporate, leaders were taught that it was not their responsibility to motivate people, but to fire those who couldn't motivate themselves. How wrong was that? Don't be fooled. Motivating your team and creating an environment where excitement, energy, and rewards are constants is critical to achieving great performance. Remember: it takes more than a paycheck to keep people engaged. Motivation and creating an exciting atmosphere are part of that "more."

Part of the Bigger Picture

Leaders are needed at every level. I can't say that I understand why people think of leadership in terms of position. Leadership has nothing to do with position or title, but rather everything to do with influencing others to take action that positively advances a cause—any cause. Hybrid leaders embrace their responsibility to the organization. They know that the only way to be in control of the future is to create it.

A hybrid leader is responsible to the organization for

✓ Leading positive and needed organizational change

✓ Advocating for company-wide work/life balance policies and nontraditional benefits

✓ Attracting, developing, and retaining top talent

✓ Promoting diversity of all types

✓ Creating collaborative teams

✓ Fostering an environment where innovation is a common thread

✓ Adding value to advance the company's vision

Getting (and Keeping) Top Talent

Despite the report released by the U.S. Labor Department regarding a skilled-labor shortage, most companies are totally clueless. Even if they know about the skilled-labor shortage, they aren't doing anything about it. When the market does turn around, and it will, employees who feel like they have been mistreated will leave. Do you know where they will go? They will seek to build a relationship with an organization where they feel welcomed, valued, needed, inspired, and fairly compensated. I am pleading with anyone who is reading this and in a position of authority to immediately do a succession review to determine who has the capability and desire to take on higher levels of responsibility. Assess your risks. Don't wait for the pain to be so great that the available medicine can't cure your illness in this area. As the Herman Group, a consulting group that studies workforce trends, said in its monthly e-zine, "Forward-thinking human resource executives guided by the executive suite will change the way they attract, screen, select, and hire employees. Long-term careers will be emphasized, a dramatic difference from tradition." Terry J. van der Werff suggests that "there will be a growing shortage of younger workers: for the next quarter century every state will grow 20%–30% faster than the number of its younger workers." The bottom line? Companies will have to invest in their people and then find ways to keep them, not lose them to the competition.

In *Her Corner Office*, I touched on the importance of organizations becoming more focused on revamping their policies and procedures to support the nontraditional needs of the twenty-first-century workforce. I cited needs such as flexible work schedules, paternity leaves, telecommuting, and job sharing. Let me share what I didn't know then but know now. According to Roger Herman, CEO of the Herman Group, one-third of all gainful employment will take place in the home by 2015. That's right around the corner, folks. Let me now expand nontraditional needs to include things like elder care, counseling, and spiritual support. Nontraditional needs may even include spousal support for men when a female employee is promoted and her husband chooses to leave behind a great career. Travel? Why, when you can use video conferencing equipment? Obviously, when face-to-face meetings are needed you'll get yourself on an airplane. But long gone are the days when people traveled for the sake of traveling. People want more time to spend with their families.

Retirement? What retirement? Another nontraditional need will be the support of baby boomers who will seek purpose and meaning in the workplace as they remain in their careers longer, which means benefits have to change. Alternative work arrangements for this segment of the workforce will become the norm. According to the *Harvard Business Review* (On Point) article entitled, "The Alternative Workplace: Changing Where and How People Work," by Mahlon Apgar IV, managers need to work through the myths and misconceptions to determine if their organization has the capability for embracing alternative schedules. The article listed seven questions for the reader to ponder in an effort to assess the company's position of readiness to deal with alternative workplaces. To me, the most interesting question was the first one: "Are you committed to new ways of operating?" What a great question! Meeting the nontraditional needs of the twenty-first-century workforce will require that every company ask and answer that question.

What about your company? Are you still an organization that rewards face time instead of results? Is your compensation system still based upon an old model that needs to be revamped? Do you know how much your organization stands to gain if your employees working in field offices worked instead from their homes? These kinds of questions need to be addressed sooner rather than later if your company is to experience success in the twenty-first century. Hybrid leaders need to do the research and present fact-based business cases to senior executives demonstrating the sense of urgency in addressing nontraditional needs as a competitive advantage. Don't wait for someone else in the organization to sound the bell in this most critical area; embrace your role as a key stakeholder of the future.

Diversity Redefined for the Twenty-first Century

When you think of diversity, what comes to mind? You might answer black, white, male, female, or minorities. To those answers, I would say that you are on the right track. But diversity in the twenty-first century means so much more. It means inclusion. It means valuing each employee for his or her uniqueness, period. Uniqueness encompasses every facet of thought, feeling, action, approach, appearance, and desire. Your employees are diverse, and so are your consumers. We know that Asian and Hispanics are the fastest-growing ethnic groups in the United States. Is your company prepared to meet their needs?

The culture of an organization reflects its beliefs, its values, and its communication practices. The dynamics of making cultural changes are enough to give you a headache. But in order to create an environment where people believe they are valued for the work they contribute and for their uniqueness, a leader has to be willing to examine and reshape, if necessary, the culture of the organization.

Creating inclusive cultures has been a challenge for organizations since the early 1980s. Companies are still trying to find the right formula even as we begin the twenty-first century. You would think it would be so simple. Can't we all just work together in peace and harmony? Can't we celebrate differences instead of seeing them as negative or just tolerating them?

Progressive leaders understand that in order to foster an environment where innovation and creativity can thrive, there needs to be diversity. When you bring together to collaborate people who are different, the team members must be able to establish meaningful relationships with each other. When you have a relationship with someone, then you are more likely to open yourself up, give that person the benefit of the doubt, and listen to other ideas. In environments where individuals are empowered to be their true selves, these types of relationships can support and respect different ways to approach and think about the business.

Creating a place where each employee can thrive and perform at his or her best is what inclusion is all about. Employees want to be respected and valued for the contribution they make to the performance outcomes of the team. If an employee feels rejected or put down because of differences, he or she disconnects from the team; the ultimate impact is negative.

Think of it this way: We may have arrived at the same company on different roads, but we are all together now! *We are the company.* There is no "them" or "they" (a group of people that are generally referred to as the ones who make stupid decisions); "they" are us. Don't pretend you haven't heard yourself saying, "Can you believe what they did this time?" That's the "they" I'm talking about. "They" don't exist. Hybrid leaders must get everyone to understand that each individual's uniqueness and the full engagement of that uniqueness make each employee valuable.

Breaking the Silos

It has long been my position that passionate and progressive thinkers working collaboratively can accomplish great things.
—Jeff Joyner

The leader's responsibility is to set the tone so that an inclusive environment can thrive. Once the tone is set, the leader needs to continue to find new ways to prevent the team from settling into subgroups or mini power partnerships (better known as silos). The leader needs to be the catalyst for implementing ground rules that reinforce positive communication between all team members and that also support best-practice processes.

These two elements will not only enhance the team's ability to create an inclusive environment, but they will help to create pockets of flexibility. These pockets of flexibility enable the team to be quick and agile in responding to new situations.

Hybrid leaders believe that valuing people, open communication, clarity of vision, and cross-functional understanding of the business creates the best environment for collaboration to occur. This type of leader believes in collaboration because the unique contributions of an extremely diverse and changing workforce must be celebrated and combined in order for an organization to achieve maximum performance. To hybrid leaders, the team is interdependent. Hybrid leaders have the ability to create an environment where individual mastery can be achieved to enhance group output. In other words, these leaders can strategically build on the skills of each team member to enrich the overall team efforts. The old model of "leader knows best" is outdated and no longer appropriate for an environment where the opportunity to achieve breakthrough results comes from collaboration. In fact, collaborative cross-functional stretchpoint teams are the teams that truly make things happen. Developing these teams is such an important goal for the hybrid leader that the next chapter is dedicated entirely to this practice.

Innovation

Consumers have changed dramatically. They have more choices and have more power than ever before. Beyond instant gratification, consumers have now moved into the "total service now and in the future" mind-set. Organizations need strong leaders who can inspire others to become more creative and innovative to meet the demands of these consumers. Noel Tichy, a leadership guru, puts it this way: "In the future, the real core competency of companies will be the ability to continuously and creatively destroy and remake themselves to meet customer demands." Diversity of approach to the business will be critical to successfully address the needs of twenty-first-century consumers.

That concept and Tichy's statement scare many people. There is no need to be scared. In fact, we should be excited.

Creativity is a skill that is inside each and every one of us. It simply must be encouraged instead of shut down. Innovation and creativity come from the richness of diversity. Diversity of thought brings creativity to life. How boring and tasteless would a cake be if it only had eggs and flour? The sugar and spices make the cake sweet, rich, and different. The importance of embracing diversity cannot be overemphasized. I wonder what kind of responses you'd get if you ask your employees to define diversity?

Everyone from top to bottom must seek innovation, and it needs to be a free-flowing element. In other words, an approach to innovation can't be that "if an employee doesn't contribute one new idea a week, then he or she will be fired." Many years ago when I was in the corporate world, I was a part of a great program focused on quality improvement. The program was designed to involve all employees in identifying ways that we could improve business processes, strategies, and approaches. It was a great program, that is, until the senior leadership started competing to see whose department would have the most entries. The ideas became absolutely ridiculous.

Environments where innovation is encouraged by way of incentives drive the wrong kind of behavior. Innovation requires a disciplined approach. Plus, the setting has to be right. I believe this is where real-time learning and permission to experience controlled failure play a role.

Innovation will drive breakthrough performance going forward. Organizations must challenge themselves to understand the changing needs of the consumer, but they must accept that, as their knowledge grows, their company will grow and change as well. Innovation is defined as acting in a new or different way, or introducing something new. But as we've already learned, most people don't like "new" because it requires change. However, innovation is essential for an organization to experience success in the twenty-first century. Coming up with great ideas is not enough; ultimately the leader has to be able to influence the team and the organization to act upon those ideas.

My favorite business case study to cite as a demonstration of what can happen when an organization is not keeping up with the trends or being led by people who have a passion for future growth is Sears. Remember when Sears was "the" store? It's a gross oversimplification to say that the failure of Sears to innovate caused the company market share, position, and profits to plummet. No one could convince the senior leadership of the Sears Corporation that there could be another business model. They honestly believed that they could maintain their number-one position, no matter what. In the next chapter Ill spend more time extracting the lessons made possible by Sears If history is any teacher, every organization that wants to succeed in the new millennium should be challenging itself to think about what the consumer will look like in five years and then make the necessary adjustments. Where will your organization be in ten or twenty years? Have you thought about it? Have you planned for the future? Can you accept that we create the future every day?

Advancing the Company's Vision

Warm bodies do nothing to advance the business. People who show up with no emotional connection, no buy-in for the vision, no ownership, or no desire might as well not be there. They are taking up space. These people are energy drains that negatively impact the rest of the group. The bottom line is results. What we have focused on during this chapter is how we get the results. Like it or not, the relationship that you have with the organization is about advancing the company's vision through extraordinary results. The company (ideally) gives you a paycheck, a great environment, respect, advancement opportunities, and appreciation, and in return you must be focused on consistently achieving great results. That's the relationship. It is a two-way street. People who don't want to live by the principles offered above are opening the door to dissatisfaction, unhappiness, and perhaps even depression.

Leadership is for the person who is willing to be a servant and embrace an enormous amount of responsibility. Leadership is a process that must be responsive to the changing business environment and the current needs of the workforce. The hybrid leader offers the best chance for significant impact in these areas. What will the situation look like tomorrow? If the futurists are on target, the best leaders of tomorrow will be behaving like hybrid leaders, attracting and keeping the best employees and anticipating the changing needs of consumers.

CHAPTER 6

Building Teams the Hybrid Leader Way

Your mind stretched to a new idea never goes back to its original dimensions.
—Oliver Wendell Holmes

Working for a Common Goal

Twenty-first-century companies must develop collaborative cross-functional stretchpoint teams. Why? Input and creative thinking from every employee are needed to discover new business models that can be the catalyst for growth. This focus on teams requires a paradigm shift for most companies. In the twentieth century the focus was placed on individual achievements, but the single-achievement model has become obsolete. Going forward, it won't be enough for organizations to maintain teams that have the mentality of going through the motions. Teams will need leaders who can guide them to reach their full potential.

In today's fast-paced, competitive environment, effective team performance is increasingly important to the success of any organization. The emotional energy can either build up or drain the output of the team. After researching many breakthrough teams to determine what common threads lie within them, I have discovered the following nine characteristics:

1. The team shares a common vision.

2. The team has a common set of guidelines that guides their daily interaction.

3. Every member of the team knows how he or she is connected to the outcome.

4. The team has a burning desire to achieve something that no other team has before.

5. The team values innovation and creativity as a critical part of the strategic planning process, and everyone brings these traits to the table.

6. The team is willing to learn in real time, understanding that no book will guide them through territory that has never before been explored.

7. The team understands that everyone brings something to the table, that each and every person should be respected for his or her individual contributions, and that they have processes to leverage all this unique power.

8. The team understands that setbacks are the foundation of resiliency.

9. The team believes in having fun and celebrating small achievements.

Step One: Collaborative Teams

In an economically pressured business world, everyone is expected to do more with less. Doing more with less requires innovation and a new approach to the business. Today's leader must be equipped and committed to developing collaborative teams. The leader has to be able to shape a framework that facilitates buy-in for continuous change and for continuous team evolution. Leaders of the twenty-first century must be capable of helping teams generate new understanding in ways never previously considered. Building collaborative teams will provide a connection between individual performance and the organization's overall goals. These teams will bring forth new best practices that will result in better internal and external partnerships, which will translate into new business-building opportunities.

Step Two: Collaborative Cross-Functional Teams

Collaborative cross-functional teams are replacing the once deeply rooted, bureaucratic, top-down management lines. These teams work across departmental boundaries to solve problems from a different perspective. In fact, in a world where change is the norm, capitalizing on collaborative cross-functional teams will separate the successful from the unsuccessful. Creating cross-functional teams requires an organization willing to eliminate departmental silos, improve communication and information sharing, and build authentic relationships that foster team cohesion, shared responsibility, and accountability.

Step Three: Collaborative Cross-Functional Stretchpoint Teams

The complex demands of today's business environment and the consumer will be the catalysts for developing collaborative cross-functional stretchpoint teams that function interdependently. The stretchpoint aspect of these teams will be the source of innovative breakthroughs, enabling companies to meet and exceed consumer expectations.

Collaborative cross-functional stretchpoint (CCFS) teams are made up of individuals from various departments within an organization who form a team to meet challenges and solve real business problems that enhance the organization's ability to be successful. These team members are committed to best-practice sharing, exchanging information and ideas, and making procedural improvements to support organizational efficiencies, innovation, and strategy execution.

What's so different about collaborative cross-functional stretchpoint teams versus regular teams? CCFS teams are the outcome of leaders removing territorial and other barriers that block team success. CCFS teams are developed through true empowerment with accountability. After senior leadership has established the organization's strategy, these teams are charged with designing programs that are innovative and effective in achieving breakthrough results.

Quantum Performance Leaps: Creating Stretchpoint Teams

Every team has a culture. In fact, within an organization you'll find as many cultures as there are leaders of teams. The culture of a stretchpoint team is unique, rooted in several critical elements. These elements include:

- Respect for the experience and expertise that each member brings to the table.

- A sense of family: Members connect with each other and are willing to take responsibility for the other person's success or failure.

- Building on each other's ideas instead of tearing them down. Team members live in a world of possibility.

- A burning desire to make a difference.

- A philosophy that shouts, "It's not about me, it's about we."

- Trusting each other.

- Empowering each other.

- Holding each other accountable.

- Willingness to be vulnerable.

Stretchpoint teams are great at having one eye on the present and one eye on the future. These teams are learning teams, and each member is committed to excellence. Creating learning teams requires behavioral changes, but these teams are capable of utilizing their diverse backgrounds, experiences, thought processes, and approaches to the business to create innovative ideas for the company.

The Power of a Common Vision

Have we not heard it enough? If you don't know where you are going, you will end up somewhere, but where is anybody's guess. As much as we have been told about the power of creating a clear vision, most managers and leaders have not done so. They have rested on the corporate vision, and they think that's enough. Wrong, absolutely wrong! A team that can connect its own team vision into the bigger vision achieves breakthrough results. The best teams relate to the organization's vision by defining how their work increases value to the customer.

The vision for the team has to be simple and teachable. Organizations and teams have spent thousands, even millions of dollars on expensive consultants to come up with just the right wording for their vision statement, but then employees can't repeat it. No wonder there is a disconnect between the team's performance and the expected outcome. If you don't believe in the power of setting a real vision, ask five people on your team a simple question: "What's our team's vision?" You'll discover what a lot of managers and leaders have discovered. You'll get five different answers. Some of the answers might be close, but not close enough to ensure that every team member is reading from the same script.

Take a look at this example of a mission statement for stretchpoint teams:

Create the product, idea, or strategy that guarantees our company's current and future success.

Without question this team is focused on innovation. But shouldn't every team be focused on innovation? Yes, but the stretchpoint team takes it to a higher level. Driving breakthrough performance is their life.

Vision statements at the team level should be fluid enough to accommodate business changes but solid enough to provide clear direction on the importance of the work. The statement above does that, balancing current realities with future opportunities. What do you think would happen if you placed this statement at every computer monitor, and in every breakroom, and talked about it at every meeting? Do you think that something good would come as a result?

Real-Time Learning

We are living in times where history isn't always the final predictor of the future. Can you say "technology"? Doesn't every generation believe that history wasn't a valid predictor for them? Perhaps each generation could find a rationale to support this belief, but the truth of the matter is that the twenty-first century truly is unlike anything that has ever happened before. Last year I took my daughter to college registration. The dean shared the following statement with the audience: "By the time that your son or daughter becomes a senior, what they learned as a freshman will be out of date." That didn't exactly fill me with a warm and fuzzy feeling, given the financial investment that I was about to make over the next four years, but that's how fast things are changing. What are some of the significant trends and drivers?

- The global economy
- The most diverse workforce in history
- Ever-changing technology
- Emerging trade channels
- Changing and unpredicted consumer purchase patterns (24/7 purchase options)

- Nontraditional work sites redefining the workplace
- New ways of obtaining education (online, distance learning)
- Self-led work teams
- A contingent workforce
- No retirement

These are just a few of the changes that are forcing today's leaders and teams to practice real-time learning. Real-time learning is just that: the ability to draw on your skills, values, and beliefs to make quick decisions in an environment of constant change. Real-time learning blows the traditional organizational hierarchy to the moon. Why? Because CEOs don't have all the answers; neither do senior vice presidents or leaders in general. Someone in the mailroom might just have the next big idea that will make the company millions of dollars. Now it is imperative to create an environment where employees at all levels feel valued enough to offer up new ideas. Real-time learning means acquiring new knowledge daily, adding on to current knowledge, and finding new ways to use the knowledge that we already have.

To optimize real-time learning, leaders must recognize that what worked yesterday will probably not work tomorrow. Unless we position ourselves to quickly adapt by not holding on to old thought patterns and old ways of approaching the business, opportunities will pass us by. As a result, stretchpoint teams are always in test mode. They aren't afraid to try something new.

Organizations that are not willing to redefine themselves will be left in the dust by the competition. Think about the growth of Wal-Mart. For years the retail industry was dominated by Sears. Whatever you needed, Sears had it. Obtaining a position of dominance caused this organization to get locked into thinking that the consumer would never change, and therefore the company didn't need to change. Then a little company called Wal-Mart came to the table and began to redefine the shopping experience. Wal-Mart's management created one-stop shopping.

They took the Sears model and added efficiency and low prices, and voila—a new way of doing business was born. Wal-Mart didn't wait for the model to be established so that they could follow it. They created the model that everyone else is now trying to follow. How did they do it? They optimized real-time learning. Wal-Mart is relentless in its pursuit of redefining the shopping experience. Every day they are engaging in test activities throughout the world, looking to create the next new model.

When Wal-Mart embarked upon redefining the shopping experience, they were not the industry leader. It's important to understand that nothing was in place to suggest the Wal-Mart model would work. After all, Sears, and to some degree Montgomery Ward, had the market nailed down. Yet through innovation, creativity, problem solving, and risk taking, Wal-Mart was able to create the new model.

This phenomenon continues to emerge as more and more retailers are building alliances to redefine their offerings. Think about gas stations that once only provided car service. Now you stop for gas and you can pick up wine, lottery tickets, bread, and just about anything else. Several retailers are considering airports as a new point of contact for customers. Dell has already leaped into this game, placing kiosks in airports. Even 7-Eleven is reportedly evaluating placing a store in an airport as a marketing test. The bottom line is that companies that are willing to extend themselves and adopt a permanent learning and testing mentality will be the winners. Organizations that do not heed the warning are at risk of being put out of business.

Reinventing the Rules

"Empowered" is such an overused word, but it is exactly how I would describe these teams. Empowerment to a stretchpoint team means autonomy plus accountability. This combination is what creates ownership. Noel Tichy, Harvard business professor and author of many books, including *The Teachable Organization*, puts it this way: "The way people get aligned is by having ownership together." Empowerment also paves the way for the team to engage in creative problem solving. Collaborative cross-functional stretchpoint team development will be a great source of motivation for employees. In order to form CCFS teams, leaders will have to give their employees real empowerment, not lip-service empowerment. I believe that this approach translates into creating an environment where everyone has a very clear understanding of the objective. They truly buy in to the objective, and they feel a sense of ownership for the outcome. CCFS also means giving people the space to use their knowledge and talents in the way that promotes the best results. Effective leaders will have to learn to get out of the way and trust that people will do the right thing. Employees want to be given the benefit of the doubt instead of having someone standing over their shoulder, walking them through step by step. Employees need space to be innovative and creative. This is the only way that productivity can increase. By releasing creative energy, new models of business will be discovered.

Of course, to empower a team the organization has to provide the team with the resources it needs to successfully execute. Some organizations have proven themselves to be more adept than others at creating ownership climates. Whole Foods is an example of an organization that has been able to create employee entrepreneurs. Whole Foods rejects the traditional top-down management style in favor of decentralization. Each employee (they actually call their employees "team members") is encouraged to make good decisions and be innovative, but they are held accountable for their actions. To help team members make good decisions, senior leadership provides financial insight, trends, margins, and other business information that serves to drive the entrepreneurial spirit. Team members have access to salary information. There is total transparency and no hidden agendas. Guess what? Whole Foods is the fastest-growing supermarket chain in the country. Maybe this empowerment-with-accountability thing works!

Real empowerment is gained through knowledge and information. As a result, organizations have to be more forthcoming with information about strategy development, profitability, legal issues or concerns, trends, and so on. Information has to be free-flowing throughout the organization, which will prove to be a huge challenge for senior executives who like having sole access to knowledge because it makes them feel powerful. Closed-door meetings, with the exception of human resource activity, should be prohibited. More often than not, in my experience, closed-door meetings are a distraction that hinders productivity and drains valuable energy as everyone wonders what is being discussed behind that closed door.

In his book *Side by Side Leadership*, Denis A. Romig brings forth research that establishes the benefits of empowering others and creating collaborative teams. He suggests that in companies where workers and leaders abandon old-style, top-down behavior and begin to share leadership, performance improves by 15 percent within six months. He also substantiates the notion that productivity improves from collaboration in his assessment of teams where leaders led their team using a side-by-side leadership style. For these teams, quality, cost control, customer satisfaction, productivity, and profits rose by 20–40 percent within one year.

In my early years of being a manager, I completely bought in to the notion that only managers should have the knowledge, not employees. It took years before it dawned on me that this concept was absolutely stupid. I learned this lesson from one of my employees. I was working in the field checking retail outlets with one of the territory sales managers who reported to me. I have never been good at hiding my feelings, and my concerns about the business were obviously showing on my face. Vincent, the sales manager, turned to me and said, "You know, you don't have to carry the load all by yourself. That's what the team is for. Let us know what's going on, and maybe we would be more willing to help."

I had always thought the leader should be the one with the worries, and that worries should not be shared because they would take away from the focus on the tasks that needed to be done. I was absolutely wrong! I learned that shared leadership is great. Once I changed my way of thinking, the ideas of the team just started flowing. We would have brainstorming sessions to address a particular issue or opportunity. The sum of the team's focus was absolutely fantastic. I began treating my employees as partners, and they began to think of me not as the boss but as their partner. We experienced breakthrough performance as a result.

Work Hard, Play Hard, Then Celebrate

Since I am a recovering workaholic, I feel I must address the value of a team pausing to engage in celebration and fun. People want work to be fun, and it should be fun! Where do you spend the majority of your waking hours? Yes, at work! So then why shouldn't we give ourselves permission to celebrate and play once in a while? Evidence suggests that teams are more productive when they give themselves permission to make work fun.

Fun and humor can be a great support mechanism to help individuals and teams overcome setbacks. Having fun and laughing are part of being resilient. Maintaining a positive outlook and a great attitude are critical components of successful teams being able to deal with the daily pressures that affect us all. When you give yourself permission to insert a little humor every now and then, you'll be more relaxed and your performance will actually improve. Stretchpoint team leaders encourage laughter because they realize that laughter, much like music, crosses all cultures, all experiences, and both genders. Laughter and fun can create wonderful memories that provide your team with a sense of connectivity and belonging. Laughing at yourself gives others permission to laugh as well.

The next time you go into an office, notice if people are smiling. Check out the noise level. Do people even talk to one another? See if you can feel the tension that floats around these employees like a haze. Then find a team that you know enjoys expressing itself in a humorous way and notice the difference. You'll find that the team who shares ultimately cares, and teams that care are able to achieve breakthrough results. It seems so obvious: if you are happy about coming to work, you'll engage more and produce more.

Southwest Airlines is an organization known for having fun. In an industry that has been hit hard by the economy and the events related to September 11, 2001, Southwest Airlines remains profitable. Their margins are reportedly the highest in the industry. The CEO has a theory that happy people are productive people. The business model works for them and can work for any other organization that is willing to create a culture where people enjoy working. Go to the Southwest Airlines Web site and look at the comments made by real employees. Their comments tell the story of why they work for Southwest. Southwest has regular celebrations where employees get together for Spirit parties and weekly deck parties at the headquarters in Dallas. These parties include activities that some would consider "childish," such as dance contests, talent shows, and karaoke. What kind of parties does your organization have? How much fun do you have on a daily basis?

Some companies are even starting to ask prospective employees about how they would use humor to help manage conflict. I believe that in the future an organization's point of difference will be connected to employee satisfaction. The best word-of-mouth marketing comes from employees inside your organization. Have you ever asked your employees how they feel about marketing the company they work for? I wonder what they would say.

PART 3

THE BENEFITS

CHAPTER 7

The Benefits of the Hybrid Leadership Style: Case Studies

The person who risks nothing, does nothing, has nothing, is nothing and becomes nothing

—Leo Buscaglia

Yes, You Really Can Make It Work

Let me give you an example of an individual who I think exemplifies one of the critical components of being a hybrid leader. SAS was featured on *60 Minutes* for being one of the best places to work. SAS is an industry leader that just keeps breaking profit records. The *60 Minutes* segment was entitled "The Royal Treatment."

Under the leadership of Jim Goodnight, the company has as its top priority employee satisfaction. Why? Because Goodnight believes that happy employees are more productive employees, and satisfied employees are able to satisfy customers. The SAS philosophy that guides their behavior is this: "If you treat employees as if they make a difference to the company, they will make a difference to the company." If you are a SAS employee, your leader is held accountable for your development. Your leader is trained with the tools and skills needed to demonstrate behavior that sends powerful signals that you as an employee are valued, respected, and treasured! On top of all of that, SAS offers day care, doctors, car repair, counselors, gyms, and family cafeterias—all onsite. As if that wasn't enough to show you the love, each employee is offered for about three thousand dollars a thirty-thousand-dollar membership to the country club that Goodnight owns.

During the course of the 60 *Minutes* report, several employees were interviewed about why they stay with SAS when they can earn more money elsewhere. Their simple response was, "I'm so happy here. I am valued here. I make a difference here!" SAS has been featured among the 100 Best Companies to work for thirteen times (*Working Mother*), and listed in *Fortune* as one of the 100 Best Companies to Work For in America.

Goodnight is doing more than just making his employees happy. He is teaching his people how to be leaders in their own right. He is instilling great values that reflect the heart of a leader. He is affecting thousands of lives, because each of those SAS employees goes home, to church, and into the community, and they share all the principles, philosophies, and beliefs embodied in what they learn from Goodnight.

Another example of a hybrid leader is Ken Chenault, CEO of the American Express Company. Not only has this gentleman demonstrated consistent business results, but he is totally focused on how those results are achieved. Chenault became CEO in January 2001. According to an article in *USA Today* on April 25, 2005, American Express had a defining moment in 2001 in conjunction with the terrorist attacks on the World Trade Center.

According to Chenault, the events of September 11 tested the management of the company in incredible ways. How did Chenault's leadership principles serve as a catalyst for the company turning this negative experience into a positive? Chenault stuck to his leadership philosophy, which he states as "define reality and give hope." After 9/11, that's what he did. In fact, much like a hybrid leader, Chenault had his people balance the focus of both the short term and long term during this critical period. It paid off big time.

Another reason that I describe Ken Chenault as an example of a hybrid leader is because of his belief in the power of people. As stated in this same *USA Today* article, Chenault reminds his employees every day of the importance of showing respect to colleagues, business partners, and even adversaries. There is great strength in humility.

Throughout history, humans have always risen to meet the challenges of the day. They've always come through with new and innovative ways to better their lives and the world around them. The twenty-first century is no different. I am confident that at the forefront of all the changes and challenges of our time will be the hybrid leader, a leader who can awaken and ignite the individual's will to succeed.

Starbucks is a documented success, no question about it. How do they do it? Besides the great products for those of you who love the caramel macchiato, they have a commitment to their people. Starbuck's chairman Howard Schultz wrote in his book, *Pour Your Heart Into It: How Starbucks Built a Company One Cup at a Time*: "I know, in my heart, if we treat people as a line item under expenses, we're not living up to our goals and our values. Their passion is our number -one competitive advantage. Lose it, and we've lost the game." From top to bottom there is support for creating an environment where people can learn. Managers create ownership by involving their employees in key decisions. Employees are referred to and treated as "partners." The success of Starbucks lends support to the hypothesis that employees are more responsive to a leadership style that openly embraces the value of the unique contributions of each and every employee, elements of the style I call hybrid leadership.

Starbucks believes so strongly in this leadership style that diversity is the company's second guiding principle in its mission statement. The first guiding principle is to provide a great work environment and to treat each other with respect and dignity. Starbucks also values and encourages several other leadership traits, such as embracing change as an opportunity. (Starbucks engages its employees in the constant reinvention of Starbucks.) Other examples of the company's commitment to the hybrid leadership style include open communication policies, focus on and connection with its people, and a burning commitment to excellence and satisfying its customers.

Howard Schultz has always been committed to developing an employee ownership program. The program called the Bean Stock plan was born under his direction. Starbucks was the first private company to offer stock options to both full-time and part-time employees. Schultz believes that valuing the team translates into customer service that is caring and responsive, which translates into profit. His self-directed work teams at the coffee plants are contributing innovative concepts. The company has benefits that extend well beyond traditional benefits. The fact that part-time employees are entitled to participate in full health-care benefits is great, but tack on free dental and vision insurance, plus all the other perks, and you've got a team that feels extremely valued. That feeling enables Starbucks to reduce turnover, which fosters the opportunity for customer relationships to be developed at every retail outlet. This approach has been critical in advancing its position as the premier coffee location. In layperson terms, it translates into "It's cool to be seen at Starbucks."

Edward Jones is another example of an organization that builds hybrid leaders. A financial planning company that is proud to fly the banner of "employer of choice," Edward Jones was ranked the number-one place to work in 2001 and 2002. Being recognized as an employer of choice positions Edward Jones at the top of potential employees' short list. Edward Jones receives on average almost five hundred thousand applications annually.

I recently had the opportunity to participate in a Webster University Leadership Development Program. Michael Holmes, who was the former chief human resource officer for Edward

Jones, was the guest speaker. His presentation focused on the company's retention strategy. He referenced five key principles that form the Edward Jones culture: credibility, respect, fairness, pride, and camaraderie. These principles guide the leadership's beliefs and behaviors. Employees are kept informed of what's important because of the company's commitment to "need to know" communication policies. Edward Jones associates understand the company's strategy and are encouraged to ask questions about it to ensure that they have belief in and ownership of the company's strategic intent. The associates are committed to hard work, and the company has high performance expectations.

"Our leaders," Holmes said, "have a commitment to eliminate politics. We want an emotionally healthy environment where our partners can grow and produce great results. We want our people to feel good about coming to work. This is the essence of our retention strategy," he said. "People like working at Edward Jones and, in turn, they recruit others to the company.

"We have a 'we are all in this together' philosophy and practice," Holmes explained. "We believe in sharing and helping each other succeed. This belief is so strong that senior associates will often give fully developed accounts to incoming employees to get them started off on a good path." In the question-and-answer session of the presentation, someone asked how Edward Jones maintains this kind of culture. Holmes responded by saying that management is constantly in touch with its people. Internal surveys are used to ascertain a deep appreciation for how the employees of the company feel they are being treated. The surveys also ask for recommendations to improve the culture of the organization. Each leader openly embraces inclusion. The guiding belief is that the quality of a diverse workforce has a direct correlation on achieving positive results.

Edward Jones's compensation programs are aligned to eliminate group competition and encourage individual competition. There is no cap on profit sharing. There are vertical and horizontal commitments to mentoring. There are no job descriptions. The company uses responsibility descriptions instead. They believe that cross-functional experience is of paramount importance. Therefore, each associate's training and development is designed based upon the anticipated responsibilities, not the job function itself.

Holmes closed the session by saying that the senior leadership of Edward Jones wants to treat its employees the way they want their customers to be treated.

Edward Jones and Starbucks are two great examples of companies that are building leaders who display hybrid leadership characteristics. There are others, but not very many. In fact, most business environments are still extremely political and hierarchy-based. Many of the people I interviewed for this book indicated that the only reason more companies were not experiencing tremendous turnover was because of the poor economy.

Few women in CEO positions lead with strong feminine traits. Anita Roddick, owner of The BodyShop, puts it this way: "I run my company according to feminine principles . . . principles of caring; making intuitive decisions; not getting hung up on hierarchy . . . ; having a sense of work as being part of your life, not separate from it; putting your labor where your love is; being responsible to the world in how you use your profits; recognizing the bottom line should stay at the bottom." What an awesome statement! It sounds so much like a hybrid leadership style. Her organization continues to experience success under this method of leadership.

Ann Fudge was the first African American female appointed as CEO of a major corporation. She was the former chairman and chief executive officer of Young & Rubicam Brands. Y&R is one of the world's largest advertising and media services firms, with about 540 offices in 80 countries. She was appointed in 2004. In the March 29, 2004, issue of *Business Week*, Ann was interviewed about her leadership journey. One of the comments she made that stuck out in my mind related to her dedication to serving others. Ann has a mission to be a catalyst for helping people see themselves in a more positive way. How wonderful to hear a CEO talking about the importance of serving others and bringing out the best in others. Where does her philosophy regarding leadership and service come from? In a *Fortune* article Ann made a very revealing statement. She said, "Power needs to be redefined." She was referring to her belief that power should be viewed as influence, not rank. She wants to reinvent the rules. She wants to address the scorecard that was designed by, as she calls them, "the boys." Ann is doing quite well, and so is Y&R. During her first months with Y&R she focused on stabilizing the business and laying the foundation for growth, which is now coming. Her down-to-earth, committed-to-serving-others style is no doubt playing a major role in her success.

One of the most impressive interviews that I conducted during the course of the research for this book was with a gentleman from Eli Lilly, Rick Smith. Rick is a twenty-five-year Lilly veteran who had experienced significant change during his employment with Lilly. What struck me most about this interview was his insightful appreciation for the need to create a new work environment. The recommendations this gentleman offered validated the beliefs that I personally hold regarding the need for corporate America to make a transformation. He began by saying that he was happy to be able to share his perspective on the Lilly story, because it's such a great story.

Lilly, like many other companies, was once run entirely by white males. During the early '70s and '80s, the economy was booming and Lilly was growing. In fact, Lilly experienced record double-digit growth for thirty years. This resulted in the organization valuing longevity instead of performance. "Many of the leaders throughout the organization adopted an 'entitlement mentality,'" he said. In other words, they became extremely comfortable. That was the beginning of the transformation. The competition turned up the heat. Then one of Lilly's most promising product introductions went sour. The stock value of the company went down, and Lilly was ripe for the taking. It seemed to happen in the blink of an eye. One day they thought they were untouchable, and the next day they hit rock bottom. This change of events caused the company to pause and regain perspective. During this time, reality began to sink in. In order for Lilly to remain successful, major change would be required.

Under the leadership of Sidney Taurel, Rick said that the culture of the organization began to embrace moving from an entitlement organization to an earning organization. Sidney introduced a new leadership style that was based upon seven principles. The entire organization was charged with shifting their behaviors to reflect Taurel's principles. The seven principles that Rick referenced were:

1. Employees should be encouraged to pursue personal success so that they can come to work happy and capable of producing.

2. People are Lilly's greatest asset. Leaders must seek every opportunity to develop diverse talent for the future.

3. Pursuit of an external focus. Lilly must stay abreast of market trends and consumer changes and be proactive.

4. Lilly must become a learning organization where best practices are openly and freely shared.

5. Lilly must be able to implement products with speed and quality.

6. Every employee must possess a thirst for excellence.

7. Employees must model the Lilly values of integrity, credibility, and respect.

The company recognized that the workforce was changing and that their consumers were global. As a result of this realization, a formalized diversity recruitment and development program was put into place. Leaders began to be held responsible not just for producing results; they were also held accountable for how they went about producing results. In other words, leaders throughout the organization were held accountable for walking the talk.

Lilly's compensation program was reengineered to provide incentive for leaders to live by the seven principles. Managers and leaders were expected to connect and interact with their people to ensure that they understood the personal and professional value of living the principles. Rick suggested that inclusion needs to be modeled in order for it to take root at every level within the organization. "Lilly is a great company to work for," he said. "I have a sense of belonging. Most employees would say that they feel like Lilly is family. People have fun and work."

In response to my question regarding work/life balance, Rick said that leaders are held accountable for demonstrating by example. A visible demonstration of senior leadership's commitment to seeking balance is important. Saying that you're committed to work/life balance and then leaving voicemails while you are on vacation is wrong. So is expecting your people to work to the point of exhaustion. "Organizations will have to find ways to honor the entire person in order to retain top talent," said Rick. "Lilly was fortunate to have had the time to make positive change. We don't want to get comfortable ever again. In fact we have a commitment to daily seek new ways to understand the needs of the customer and take whatever actions are necessary in order to exceed customer expectation." In today's competitive environment other companies will probably not be so lucky. Those companies that don't heed the call will be left behind. Eli Lilly has been recognized by *Working Mother* magazine, *Industry Week*, and *Fortune* magazine (Best 100 Companies to Work For).

Let me offer insight on one more company that I believe is led by individuals who apply hybrid leader tenets. That company is The Container Store. Founders Kip Tindell and Garrett Boone have a unique perspective on the value of people. As called out in the hybrid leadership model, people are the company's greatest asset. This is exactly the underlying philosophy that makes The Container Store so successful. This philosophy is lived out by the people whom they choose to hire. In fact, one of The Container Store's core business philosophies is that one great person equals three good people. This company and its leaders set people up for success. How do they do it? They match an employee's strengths with the needs of the company. They also focus on talent rather than titles. What novel concepts!

Is it any wonder this company has been recognized four years running as one of the 100 Best Companies to Work For? In an industry known for extremely high turnover (the retail industry typically experiences more than 100 percent turnover) and difficulty recruiting, The Container Store breaks the mold. Tindell and Boone operate from a "do unto others" business philosophy. They refer to this as the foundation principle. Principles based on this philosophy guide their commitment to transparent communication (a key trait of the hybrid leadership style). In addition to a great culture, every employee who works eighteen hours or more is entitled to some health benefits. There are also flex hours available for employees who have children.

"A funny thing happens when you take the time to educate your employees, pay them well, and treat them as equals," president and CEO Kip Tindell declares. "You end up with extremely motivated and enthusiastic people." With a commitment like this at the top, there is no way that an organization can fail to be successful. Well, I guess you could be unsuccessful if you had a terrible product, but if you had good people, they wouldn't stand for it. The main point to take away from The Container Store example is this: they focus on the "how" of getting the results, not just getting the results.

These are just a few examples of organizations that have flourished because they have leaders who lead based upon hybrid leadership principles. Many individuals are leading based upon hybrid leadership principles and influencing their organizations to holistically adopt those principles. They will be the catalysts for transforming organizations. A few of these people are Linda Dillman, CIO of Wal-Mart; Richard Pogue, managing partner for CB Richard Ellis; Maurice Morgane; Mike Hansen and Vicki Felker of the Nestlé Purina Pet Care Company; and Rebecca Scelz of Deloitte & Touche.

I'm sure that there are many leaders in the business world who lead based upon some of these principles. Let me know who you think that they are. As I continue my research in this area and continue to refine the concept, I will no doubt benefit from interviewing others who believe as I do. Send me an email at trudy@workforceexcellence.com with your thoughts.

PART 4

MAKING THE
TRANSFORMATION

CHAPTER 8

Applying the Knowledge

The men [and women] who succeed are the efficient few. They are the few who have the ambition and will power to develop themselves.

—Herbert Casson

Put Yourself First (for the Moment)

What are your current leadership principles and philosophies? How do your current beliefs and practices differ from the hybrid leadership style? What changes do you need to make personally in order to embrace the hybrid leadership principles and philosophies? I believe that your career advancement strategy must include adopting a leadership transformation that paves the path for total acceptance of the hybrid leadership style, but before you can develop your own hybrid leader path you must do the following:

- **Completely** understand yourself and why you want to be a leader.

- **Choose** to deal with those parts of you that need definite improvement.

- **Understand and appreciate** the key differences between the behaviors of men and women.

- **Identify** which behaviors from the opposite gender you can add to your leadership style that will strengthen you.

If you have never taken the time to consider any of the aforementioned thoughts, you can refer to my first book, *Her Corner Office*, for help in self-assessment and creating a personal mission statement. Once you have thoroughly completed the steps above, then you need to examine your own leadership principles versus the leadership principles of the hybrid leader. **Warning:** In order to do this, you have to be willing to dig deep into your beliefs and find a place where you are comfortable with learning and changing your own behaviors. Several of the behaviors we have already covered in previous chapters. Those, and some that have not yet been covered, are outlined below:

Personal growth is realized through hard work and commitment. Use this matrix as a guide as you begin to identify those areas that you want to develop and fine tune.

Personal Development Matrix

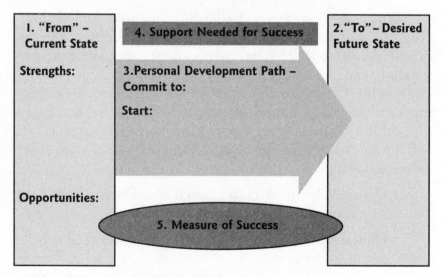

Emotional Discipline

- Be aware of how you view and react to others.

- Learn how to flex your style to gain an understanding of issues that are out of your normal purview.

- Openly express your emotions, but be sensitive to those whose positions differ.

- Embrace change as opportunity.

- Be willing to shape the social climate of the organization through verbal endorsement of new strategies.

- Manage your intensity and the intensity of the team to avoid burnout.

Decision Making

- Gather the facts.

- Consider the short-term and long-term implications of your decisions.

- Consider the risk of making no decision.

- Trust your intuition.

- Don't waffle back and forth once a decision is made.

- Recognize that there will always be someone who won't agree with your position.

- Acknowledge that you don't have all the answers and be willing to gather input to complement your own thoughts and ideas.

Overcoming Stereotypes

- Ask yourself how you would feel if your son or daughter were subjected to negative gender or ethnic stereotypes.

- Challenge yourself to embrace differences. If you demonstrate your commitment to value others, you'll be valued in return.

- Look for the good in others.

- When you revert to bad behavior, acknowledge and apologize for your behavior.

- Practice affirming the importance of others.

- Strive to eliminate barriers that limit career advancement

Work/Life Balance

- Walk the talk if you are committed to demonstrating leadership. That means having family pictures in the office and being there for important events in your children's lives.

- Support flexible work schedules for both men and women.

- Adopt a performance matrix that measures performance results, not the number of hours that an employee spends in the building.

Interpersonal Skill Development

- Commit to the highest standard of integrity, trustworthiness, and reliability.

- Learn to objectively challenge others.

- Resist monopolizing conversations and thus preventing others from contributing.

- Learn to engage others from a spirit of possibilities instead of competitiveness.

- Listen in the moment; be present and fully engaged.

- Mentor and develop future leaders as a personal best practice.

Focus on Results

- Remove obstacles that block progress.

- Look for every opportunity to celebrate small victories to build momentum.

- Develop feedback loops that are politics-free.

- Build autonomous teams with accountability for producing high results.

- Commit to setting an example rooted in excellence.

- Recognize that as the leader you must continually inspire the team to achieve results.

- Proactively respond to change by staying abreast of changes in the global business environment.

- Get comfortable with creating the future.

Valuing People

Can you imagine a business world where diversity of thought would be so highly respected that it would not be necessary for you, as the leader, to hand-hold, nor would you have the time to do so? That world is being created right now! Virtual self-directed teams will become the norm. To manage these teams, leaders will have to place special emphasis on strong communication skills.

For example, take time to appreciate the contributions of the different generations in the workforce. This approach will enrich the team, the company, and the offerings to the customers. From the youngest worker to the oldest, each has valuable information and insight based on his or her personal life experiences. Learn to listen without judgment, and determine to discover what you have in common. Find out what motivates each of your employees to give 100 percent.

The job descriptions for leaders in the new century will focus far more on relationship and change management. As a result, strong interpersonal skills will enhance your ability to connect and build the kind of relationships that will foster team development. To effectively manage and lead these virtual teams, a leader will be required to flex his or her style. In order to find a way to motivate the team, greater emphasis will need to be placed on being compassionate and helping others to achieve the highest level of productivity by aligning their passions with their jobs.

John Kotter suggests in his book *Leading Change* that organizations will become far more transparent and inclusive. The cultures that will develop in the business world will be less hierarchical and bureaucratic. The power-hungry male image of leadership will slide away to a new, more inspiring, authentic leader who values people and wants to make an impact that is greater than obtaining a six-figure income and the corner office. I believe that the good ol' boy network will be dismantled. It will be replaced with the good ol' people club as a result of demographic shifts in the workforce.

Wouldn't it be a breath of fresh air to work in an organization that is not loaded with yes people who survive day to day by trying to suck up to the boss? The strongest leaders will surround themselves with people who challenge their every move. They will gain energy and creativity from being challenged. These leadership behaviors will be the foundation for a new culture, where people will feel a sense of belonging and, as a result, generate higher levels of productivity.

What does this mean for you in your career as a leader? It means that you will need to focus on fine-tuning some very important skills, specifically:

- Communication—with a focus on listening to gain understanding for what is being said and why it is being said.

- Relationship management/interpersonal skill—being open to developing true relationships in the work environment.

- Collaborative team development—with the emphasis placed on creating a team culture where learning from each other is encouraged. Everyone's input will be valued and respected. Focus on obtaining synergies and efficiencies will be critical.

- Flexibility—becoming exceptional at connecting with people from diverse backgrounds. This will require the ability to flex "normal" behavioral styles in order to understand and extract the best from others.

Why Is Change So Difficult?

From the earlier chapters in this book, you now have a very clear picture of what the twenty-first-century worker looks and acts like. You also know that optimizing this workforce requires a new model. It requires leaders that are willing, as software company SAS CEO Jim Goodnight says, to dare to be different. That means change. The one thing that is constant today is change. I personally think that change is good. Change doesn't guarantee success, but success cannot occur without change. So often we fear change, but we won't be successful without truly embracing change as an opportunity. Even the most awful occurrences that have taken place in this world have yielded positive outcomes. Take the September 11 tragedy as an example. It certainly changed America, and perhaps the world, forever! One positive result that came out of that occurrence was that many people began to rethink their priorities. It was as if people suddenly realized that life is shorter than they thought, and spending time on what's important is a wise decision.

A vast scope of changes is spilling over into the workplace. There are changes in the demand for different types of workers, changes relative to the core competencies that are needed for success, and changes occurring with regard to how people look at their employer. Most people will work for as many as ten companies over their work life. I don't particularly believe that these constant employment shifts are beneficial to the productivity of corporations as a whole. In an article by Elayne Robertson Demby entitled "Loyalty May Become Cool Again," she suggests that as a result of baby boomers nearing retirement and company knowledge becoming more important than ever, long-term employees will become valuable once again. In this same article, a reference is made to a comment offered by Deborrah Himsel of Avon. She shares her belief that both the employee and the employer are looking at building more of a long-term relationship. Companies are now seeing that committed employees lead to increased productivity. The easiest thing to do now is to put this book down and think, "What a nice idea." The challenge I give to you is this: Put this information into action. Don't wait another minute! I've heard it said that you have seventy-two hours after you have had knowledge transferred to you to take a step to make it stick. Please take that step. You will become a better leader and person as a result. Most professionals I have observed in my twenty years of business don't make behavior changes unless prompted to do so through a negative performance, or perhaps somebody tells them that unless they make behavioral adjustments they won't get promoted. How about this as a motivator—being the best you can be because of a personal commitment to excellence. Let me use the words of a colleague and friend, Dessie Leff, who said, "Challenge by choice is yours for the taking."

To help you get started, I've given you this chapter full of leadership challenges. Using everyday issues that leaders face in the business world as the key areas of focus, I've outlined how a traditional leader would respond and then how a hybrid leader would respond. Consider this your first "hybrid leader coaching."

Leadership Challenge:
Team Performance Improvement

Hire the best. Pay them fairly. Communicate frequently. Provide challenges and rewards. Believe in them. Get out of their way and they'll knock your socks off.
—Mary Ann Allison

Question: I want to increase my team's performance. I've tried everything, but nothing seems to be working.

Traditional Leadership Model Answer: Get on a mission to fire those who can't motivate themselves immediately. Focus on the people who are doing a great job, and let the rest of the people hang themselves.

Hybrid Leader Answer: Start by following one of Stephen Covey's principles: seek to understand. You can't help others improve if you don't understand where they are currently and what is in their way of success. Don't ever give up on people who are underperforming. Match up the high performers with the underperformers, and begin to develop best practices. There are pockets of excellence in your team; bring them into the light for the benefit of the entire team. You'll be amazed at the progress that your team will make as a result.

Hybrid Leader Tips

Ask your team these simple questions:

1. What needs to change in this department in order for you to make your greatest contribution?

2. If you were in charge, what three things would you change to improve the team's performance?

3. What needs to change in your life in order for you to experience personal and professional success?

4. How can I serve you better as a leader (i.e., providing support, training, insight, or direction) to support your achievement of excellence?

5. What ideas do you have to help change the culture of this team?

Once you receive feedback, take immediate action.

Leadership Challenge:
Culture Change

Question: I want to be a leader so that I can be a catalyst for shaping organization culture. But what can I possibly do as one person?

Traditional Leadership Model Answer: The culture is set from the top. Don't stray from the tone that has already been set. You don't want to call attention to yourself for bucking the system.

Hybrid Leader Answer: Focus on the organization's culture, but keep it in perspective. If it is not a culture that you believe is right, then do something about it. Begin by focusing on your team's culture. Getting the culture of your team right is the first step at influencing the organization.

Hybrid Leader Tips

- Develop team guiding principles that everyone buys into. Every team is known for something. Incorporate your team's branding into your guiding principles.

- Provide autonomy to your team. This will serve to bring out their greatest strengths, but be sure to provide clear direction that includes what you are looking for in terms of end results.

- Create an expectation that "how" you achieve the results is as important as achieving the results.

- Be a transparent communicator. Keep your team informed of everything that is happening in the company.

- Establish clear boundaries with accountability.

- Create an environment where the team knows how their everyday contributions make a difference to the bottom line.

- Connect with your people; build relationships.

- Host an "idea" meeting monthly to infuse innovation into the natural behavior of your team.

- Establish policies and procedures that demonstrate your commitment to value the employee holistically:

  ◦ No meetings scheduled before 9 a.m.

  ◦ Don't charge for time taken for parent/teacher visits.

  ◦ Ask your human resource department to develop a list of resources for elderly care or backup child care.

- Be clear about your own understanding of how the white male culture has shaped the organization. This move will help to identify what areas need to change in order to create an environment where all employees can experience success.

Leadership Challenge:
Black Women Perceived to Be
"Angry Black Women"

Question: I find it so difficult to connect with black women. It seems to me that they are angry. I know that it's not toward me, but I don't know how to handle it. I want to help my employee perform at her best. Help!

Traditional Leadership Model Answer: Be very careful. Watch every word that you say. You don't want to invite the race card to be played. Focus on making sure that you stick to the policies and procedures that have been mandated by the company. Don't try to get to know the person; focus on the results.

Hybrid Leader Answer: Open your heart to this person. Express your concerns and fears in a true spirit of developing an authentic relationship. No matter what your race, gender, or culture is, make a human connection with this person. This will be the foundation of creating an environment where this woman can reveal her true spirit and commitment to perform with excellence.

Hybrid Leader Tips

- Make a human-to-human connection.

- Openly communicate your feelings and concerns.

- Express your total commitment to her success.

- Openly acknowledge that there is no way you can understand her "journey" but that you are willing to be a supporter.

- Share every bit of knowledge you have that will help her advance and achieve her goals.

- Give her tough feedback, but do it in a spirit of love.

- Create an environment where she feels welcomed by openly discussing race and associated perceptions among the entire team.

- Help her to find a mentor and a sponsor.

Leadership Challenge:
Innovation for Future Success

*Every tomorrow has two handles. We can take hold of it with the handle
of anxiety or the handle of faith.*

—Henry Ward Beecher

Question: I am so busy in the present that I can't even think about the future. What can I do to be more focused on success in the short term and the long term?

Traditional Leadership Model Answer: Short-term profits and success are what you need to stay focused on. Tomorrow is not promised, so live for today. Just make sure that everything you are doing today produces the best results, and tomorrow will take care of itself. Besides, if it doesn't, it won't be on your watch. You'll be long gone by then. Let the next leader worry about the future.

Hybrid Leader Answer: You are in trouble! If you don't plan for the future, you will be left out. You must take responsibility for shaping the future. It is a leader's responsibility to balance the decisions that are made for the benefit offered in both the short term and the long term. Just look at the many case studies where organizations have not prepared for the future and the competition has taken them out of the game or at least forced the organization to adopt a new business model. Think of TiVo and Blockbuster.

Blockbuster was on a winning track but took their eye off the business trends about the time DVD was being introduced. When TiVo started providing consumers with the ability to order movies online at home, Blockbuster realized they could provide similar services, woke up and began to re-brand themselves with new services, including the introduction of "no more late fees."

Like Blockbuster, you must focus on the future. You must create an environment where every decision is filtered through the short- and long-term impact. But it requires dedication and discipline. These tips will get you started on the road to success.

Hybrid Leader Tips

Spend time weekly (what I call white space) thinking about the future.

Write down your thoughts and concerns about the future.

Give yourself and your team permission to play with the future (What if we did . . . ?).

Keep your finger on the pulse of significant trends that could impact your business.

Look for the problems or opportunities that you think your consumer will have five, ten, or twenty years out, and then brainstorm about the product or service you can provide that will offer the solution.

Leadership Challenge:
Personal Growth

No one is responsible for your destiny except you. If you want greatness, reach for it.
—Trudy Bourgeois

Question: I am so busy developing my people that I don't have time to develop myself.

Traditional Leadership Model Answer: Take a couple of classes; you'll be fine. Learn from the network; these people are full of great insights.

Hybrid Leadership Answer: Recognize that as you develop others, you develop yourself. But don't rely on that in totality. You can definitely learn from the network, but what about those people who are not in the network? That might just be you. Take ownership of your development. Create your own plan, and adopt a thirst for continuous learning and growth.

Hybrid Leader Tips

Learning comes in all shapes and sizes. It appears when you least expect it. "When the student is ready, the teacher will appear." Keep your eyes, ears, and heart open for learning. Often it is just a matter of making a mental shift about the way you can learn. These steps will help.

- Conduct a personal assessment (there are plenty of great assessment tools).

- Focus on refining your strengths.

- Set a goal to learn one new thing every day.

- Start a mastermind group that reviews the top business books.

- After every project is completed, engage in a postmortem review. Ask yourself what could have been done better to improve the results, and then seek the knowledge that will allow you to do that next time.

- Identify role models and interview them to understand their skill sets.

Leadership Challenge:
Change

Change is an opportunity for those who are willing to move beyond managing it to embracing it.

—Trudy Bourgeois

Question: Change is one of the most pressing challenges I face as a leader. How do I deal with it myself, and how do I help my people deal with it?

Traditional Leadership Model Answer: People don't like change, so don't beat yourself up. There is no easy answer to this question. Remind people that they are lucky to have a job, and they just need to suck it up and deal with it.

Hybrid Leadership Answer: Change is difficult for people. Your role is to make your own paradigm shift first to a place where you are not just managing change but embracing it. You need to get to a place where you are excited about change because of the opportunities that it opens. You are the role model for your team, so if you are resisting change so will they. Change is about emotions first and foremost, not logic. You've got to help your people realize that change is a fundamental part of life. In fact, it is the birthright to continued future success.

Hybrid Leader Tips

- Read John Kotter's *The Heart of Change.*
- Make sure that people understand the reason behind the change that is occurring.
- Openly acknowledge that change is difficult, but then brainstorm with your team on change that they have experienced that was positive to help them build a new baseline for associating change with something positive.

- Convey to your people the link between future success and their willingness to be flexible and adaptive (two critical points for excellence in the twenty-first century).

- Point out the critical changes that are driving new business models around the world.

- Give people permission to challenge everything, to seek a new way to make it better. This will encourage people to want to seek out change.

- Help your team to see that change provides a great opportunity for learning.

- Seek to formulate a mental state that change is an ongoing journey.

Leadership Challenge:
Retaining Great Bench Strength

Question: How should I go about conveying the essence of the company's succession planning process so that I can keep my top talent and increase my bench strength?

Traditional Leadership Model Answer: You don't want to make any promises you can't keep. It isn't wise, therefore, to share the company's succession plans with the team. You can certainly share that there is a succession planning process, but don't get into specifics.

Hybrid Leader Answer: If you want to keep your good people, tell them what the succession plans are. Don't ever build a succession plan and then keep it secret. It only invites speculation and unnecessary turnover. Make sure that you communicate that this is a plan, not a guarantee. The individuals who have been identified on the plan must meet expectations. Many top performers leave organizations because they don't see opportunity for advancement. But they will stay if they know they are valued and considered to be a part of the next generation of leaders for the organization.

Hybrid Leader Tips

- Be transparent about the entire succession planning process.
  - How does a person get on the list?
  - What do you have to do to stay on the list?
  - How is the plan aligned with the organization's future?
  - How is the plan aligned with the individual's personal desires?
- Openly communicate what you see as the highest level of responsibility that each member of your team can achieve. Don't exaggerate; be as candid as possible.
- Make sure that what the company views as opportunities aligns with the employees' career vision.
- Remove subjectivity from the process. Enlist the aid of a competency-based assessment.
- Review annually the competencies that are identified to ensure that they are aligned with the short- and long-term needs of the business.
- Make sure that the succession plan accounts for the dynamics of a changing workforce where older workers are staying in the organization longer.
- Help your employees see the value in cross-functional training.
- Explain that successful careers run sideways and upwards and include all kinds of stretch assignments.

- Make sure that the individuals you deem appropriate for higher levels of responsibility are willing to invest in themselves as much as the company is willing to invest in them.

Leadership Challenge:
Inclusion

We'll know when we have achieved our inclusion goals when we no longer have to talk about it.

—Vicki Felker

Question: My organization talks a good game about inclusion, but the executive team is all white men. I am struggling to determine if the organization is really serious about inclusion. How can I serve up my concerns in a positive way?

Traditional Leadership Model Answer: There is so much confusion about diversity and inclusion that I would recommend you wait until the dust settles before taking any steps. Make sure that your team has been through all the diversity training programs so that you can check it off.

Hybrid Leader Answer: Your organization is, at best, fairly superficial regarding inclusion. Take the time to dig a little deeper. It could be that there are people of color in the pipeline who are on the short list to get to the executive level. You certainly should engage in a fruitful dialogue with your immediate manager about the company's plans to ensure that the entire management team reflects the face of the consumer. During that conversation you can express your sincere desire for the organization to make visible progress in this area, but make sure that you have challenged yourself to clarify how you feel about inclusion.

Hybrid Leader Tips

- Reflect on your own beliefs and behaviors regarding inclusion.

- Show courage by openly communicating your personal beliefs.

- Influence and persuade others by your actions as a leader.

- Take a look at your own team. Is it diverse? Before you start talking about the wider organization, make sure that your house is in order.

- Talk openly with your team about why inclusion is so important to the business and to their individual contribution and advancement.

Leadership Challenge:
Conflict

Question: I have the worst time getting people to successfully deal with conflict. How can I help my people to move beyond conflict into collaboration?

Traditional Leadership Model Answer: Competition is natural. Let them agree to disagree and encourage them to move on.

Hybrid Leader Answer: Healthy competition is both natural and good. Conflict is also natural because people have different opinions and viewpoints. What is unacceptable is not getting to a place of mutual agreement. Try these steps to address the situation:

Hybrid Leadership Tips

- Foster an environment where people can openly express their feelings and opinions.

- Make sure that the ground rules are clearly understood, i.e., don't attack the person, only the idea.

- Invite those in conflict to focus on creating a new idea by blending the best of all the ideas.

- Invite those in conflict to remove the emotional investment so that they can see the opportunity from a different standpoint.

- Teach your employees how to listen with an ear for possibility.

- Create a new level of ownership and commitment for the outcome that results from working through the conflict.

Leader Challenge:
Ambiguity

Question: As a minority, I feel like I don't know where I stand in the company. I can't seem to find my footing.

Traditional Style of Leadership Answer: What are you talking about? We're all the same here. You have as much chance to get ahead as anyone.

Hybrid Leader Answer: Ambiguity is a way of life in the corporate world. Most leaders are just more likely to promote employees of their same race. Your focus first needs to be on the career path you want, then look and see how you can get there from here.

Hybrid Leader Tips

- Coach the employee to avoid the pitfalls of trying to play the "political game." Leave politics to the politicians.

- Advise the employee to develop good coping skills. Help him to be confident in what he has to offer and to not take criticism personally.

- Help the employee find role models, either internally or externally, from the same culture.

- Help the employee get connected with an affinity group, or help start one.

- Draw on the human resource department for support.

Leadership Challenge:
Women at the Top

Question: So much emphasis has been placed on women and developing women for senior leadership positions that the rest of my team is starting to become resentful. What can I do to help people understand why it is important to value women as strong business leaders?

Traditional Leadership Model Answer: Well, tell them that it's because we need a few women at the top to help balance things out. Tell them to treat women like any other member of the team. If women earn the right to be viewed as credible leaders, then let them have it.

Hybrid Leader Answer: Be intentional about explaining the discrimination that women have experienced in the business world. Explain the business case (i.e., the buying power of women). If you don't know about the buying power of women, get the information. Help your employees see that many of the skills women bring to the table as leaders are the exact skills needed in today's work environments. Make sure that your female employees are given the same "automatic" leadership credibility as their male counterparts.

Hybrid Leader Tips

- Maintain zero tolerance for anyone who cannot display behaviors that demonstrate value for women as leaders.

- Host roundtable business discussions to openly talk about gender and leadership with an emphasis on helping others to understand similarities and differences (use this book as a guide).

- Host luncheons and seminars where women openly talk about the unique challenges they face.

- Explain the business case for developing women.

- Explain that is discriminatory to hold women back just because they are women.

- Help your team understand how developing strong women business leaders is tied to their future success.

Afterword

Thank you for taking the time to read my book. I know how busy life gets and what a commitment it takes to secure time to invest in your own development. I trust that as a result of reading this book you not only have new knowledge but new inspiration to get involved in leading workplace transformation.

I am sincere about my commitment to serve as a resource to help individuals, teams and organizations improve their ability to perform! I believe that we both share a passion that being to unleash the greatest potential in ourselves and in others. Nothing would please me more than to hear about your growth as you apply the principles contained in this book. Send me an email at trudy@workforexcellence.com and let me know of your successes and challenges!

And, please visit my websites www.workforexcellence.com and www.trudypresents.com to learn about upcoming workshops, seminars and special features. Also be on the look out for information about the design of a Plano based Learning Lab Studio. It is my dream to create a place where people can come to take off the workplace mask, learn and have fun! I'll let you know how things develop.

Until our paths cross again, God be with you and yours!

Trudy Bourgeois

About the Author

Trudy Bourgeois is a performance strategist who specializes in developing leaders who can elicit the greatest contribution from every employee. She teaches managers, developing leaders and executives how to create environments where every employee is fully engaged, authentic relationships support collaboration and innovation and best practices are created to support breakthrough business results.

A former sales/marketing executive who broke the glass ceiling to become one of the first African American female VP's in the consumer goods industry. Trudy has lead teams of thousands and managed budgets in the billions.

Now she is a performance and executive coach and performance strategist to many senior executives at Nestle Purina Pet Care Company, The Gillette Company, Grainger, Sara Lee and Wal-Mart. Trudy's company, The Center for Workforce Excellence, is a national traiing, coaching, and consulting firm that provides performance improvement services to global organizations. Areas of expertise include Women and Leadership, Gender and Leadership, Minority Challenges in the Workplace, Change Management, Cultural Improvement, and Team Development.

Trudy's experiential learning workshops offer business simulation models that help executives and managers change their personal behavior in a safe environment which enables clients to put theory into practice. Fueling personal growth is a core value for Trudy, who believes that a leader's greatest responsibility is to unleash the greatest potential in themselves and others. Her performance improvement models have served as catalysts for individual, team and organizational performance breakthroughs.

The devoted wife of Mike Bourgeois for twenty-five years, Trudy lives near Dallas, Texas and is the mother of two children, Adam and MaryEllen

Trudy Bourgeois
President, CEO The Center for Workforce Excellence
3941 Legacy Drive
Suite 204, #118B
Plano, TX 75023
214-387-3170 (Phone)
214-387-3180 (Fax)
www.thehybridleader.com
www.workforceexcellence.com
www.trudypresents.com

Trudy Bourgeois is a performance strategist who specializes in developing leaders who can elicit the greatest contribution from every employee

Also by Trudy Bourgeois:

Her Corner Office: A Guide to Help Women Find a Place and a Voice in Corporate America

~ ~ ~ ~ ~ ~ ~

Planning a Meeting? Visit www.trudypresents.com to find out more about Trudy speaking to your group.

For hundreds of tips on leadership effectiveness, please visit www.workforceexcellence.com.

Seven Key Hybrid Leadership Principles

Principle #1. Self-connection is the key to leveraging your hard wiring and strengths. It is also the only way to adopt new behaviors.

Principle #2. Meet your employees where they are. They are the company's greatest asset. Eliciting the greatest contribution from every employee is mission critical.

Principle #3. Build authentic relationships. Authentic connections serve as anchors for loyalty, commitment, and full engagement.

Principle #4. Become a servant. Serving is the key to harnessing the greatest of others. Humility is the first step on the path to grace.

Principle #5. Leverage emotional intelligence. Emotional intelligence is the window to leverage the uniqueness of each employee.

Principle #6. Focus on "how" results are achieved. When people are taught what to do, they are so much better than when a leader just tells them to do it.

Principle #7. Never stop learning. The keys to success in the future are flexibility, adaptability, and change. To apply these you must be willing to learn all the time.

Tips to Make the Transformation to Hybrid Leader

Tip #1. Fall in love with problems. The reason that companies need leaders and employees is to solve problems. If there is anything called "job security," it is opportunities disguised as problems.

Tip #2. Be buttoned up. Do your homework. Be prepared. Gather new knowledge on a daily basis.

Tip #3. Take personal responsibility. No victims allowed. No one can create success for you. You must choose to take action, which means taking personal responsibility and ownership for current and future situations.

Tip #4. Become a powerful influencer/persuader. Reshaping the mind-set in an effort to create an environment where every employee can thrive requires you to become a brilliant and powerful influencer.

Tip #5. Find your sales hat. If you want people to embrace your thoughts, ideas, and strategies, you've got to sell them. But it must be done in a spirit of service. Would you buy something that you didn't believe in?

Tip #6. Celebrate diversity. Diversity is found in the uniqueness of each and every person. Celebrating differences requires a deep discovery of personal beliefs and values.

Tip #7. Embrace multiple perspectives. Conflict can lead to innovation when you are willing to open yourself to see an idea from someone else's viewpoint.

Tip #8. Open your ears. Listening is the most important part of communication. To actively listen, one must be willing to be present in the moment, to be empathetic by demonstrating a willingness to validate others, and to honor them by respecting their opinions.

Tip #9. Admit you don't have all the answers. Leaders don't have all the answers. They just have the desire to find them or create them.

Tip #10. Have some fun. Life is too short to be so doggone serious about stuff that won't even matter in ten years. Move on and enjoy despite the flops, fumbles, and failures (as described by Pastor George Feiser).

APPENDIX C

Suggested Resources

www.workfamily.com

www.executivewomenpowertrack.com

www.bwni.com

www.diversitybestpratices.com

www.diversityinc.com

www.faithpopcorn.com

www.betterworkplacenow.com

www.workoptions.com

www.patrickdixon.com

www.hermangroup.com

www.newtrainingideas.com

www.hoovers.com

APPENDIX *D*

Hybrid Leader Personal Transformation Model

Accessing new behaviors doesn't just happen. Adopting a leadership style that blends the strengths of the male and female requires that you acknowledge and respect the value of the opposite gender's contributions. As you now go about the business of leading it will be easy to fall back into old habits. I challenge you not to do so. I believe that you can become a hybrid leader and I know that you and everyone that you touch will benefit from your transformation. Corporate America needs you.

Knowledge in and of itself is not powerful. It only becomes powerful when you put it into action. You have taken a big step by reading this book and acquiring new knowledge but you've got a few more steps that you'll need to commit to deploying daily. They are:

- Make the choice to expand your capabilities and acquire new behavior. This requires you to be intentional.

- Seek to acquire new knowledge that enriches your thinking, perspective, and action on the area of focus.

- Leverage "time zero." Time zero is the point at which your brain acquires new knowledge by electing not to act on prior learning and default behavior.

- Apply the new knowledge to expand your behavior choices.

- Integrate the expanded behaviors into your personal behavior tool kit and best practices.

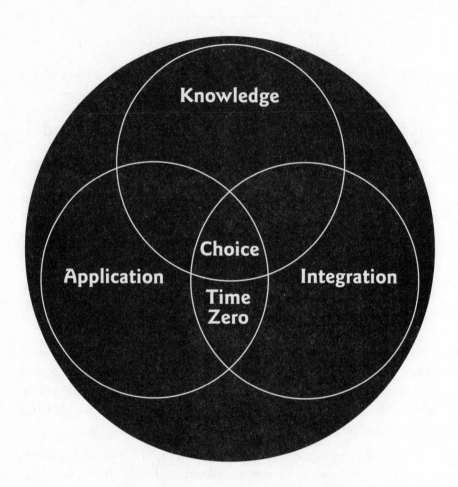

Personal Transformation Model

Selected Bibliography

Apgar, Mahlon, IV. "The Alternative Workplace: Changing Where and How People Work." *Harvard Business Review* On-Point Collection, 1998.

Brady, Diane. "Cover Story: Act II." *Business Week*, March 29, 2004.

Claes, Marie-Therese. "Women, Men and Management Styles." *International Labour Review*, December 22, 1999.

Cohn, D'Vera. "Immigrants Account for Half of New Workers." *Washington Post*, December 2, 2002.

Collins, Jim. *Good to Great: Why Some Companies Make the Leap . . . and Others Don't.* New York: HarperCollins Publishers, 2001.

"Defining Google." www.cbsnews.com/stories/2004/12/30/60minutes.

Demby, Elayne Robertson. "Loyalty May Become Cool Again." Workforce online, January 2002. www.workforce.com/section/06/feature/23/38/78/.

Drucker, Peter F. *Managing in the Next Society.* New York: Truman Talley Books, 2002.

———"They're Not Employees, They're People." *Harvard Business Review*, February 2002.

Flora, Carlin. "Do Women Make Better Leaders?" *Psychology Today*, September 17, 2003.

Giuliani, Rudolph W., and Ken Kurson. *Leadership*. New York: Miramax Books, 2002.

Helmstetter, Shad. *What to Say When You Talk to Your Self*. New York: Pocket Books, 1982.

Hollon, John. "A Simple Philosophy." *Workforce Management*. December 4, 2004.

"It's Hard Being Soft: Best of HBR on Leadership." *Harvard Business Review* OnPoint Collection, 2001.

Jones, Del. "Female Executives Display Business Savvy." *USA Today*, January 3, 2004.

Kendall, Joshua. "It's Your Problem Too." *Business Week*, Frontier, February 28, 2000.

Koch, Jennifer. "Thinking Outside the Box at The Container Store." Workforce.com, March 2001.

Kotter, John P. *Leading Change*. Boston: Harvard Business School Press, 1996.

Loden, Marilyn, and Judy B. Rosener. *Workforce America! Managing Employee Diversity as a Vital Resource*. New York: McGraw-Hill, 1990.

Miller, Marlane. *BrainStyles*. New York: Simon & Schuster, 1997.

Murrow, Lance. "The Temping of America." *Time*, March 29, 1993.

Reich, Robert B. "Your Job Is Change." *Fast Company* 39 (October 2000).

"Revote Slated Amid Carty Apology." NBC5i.com/news/2123890/detail.html, April 21, 2005.

Romig, Dennis. *Side by Side Leadership: Achieving Outstanding Results Together.* Austin, TX: Bard Press, 2001.

Rosener, Judy B. *America's Competitive Secret: Women Managers.* New York: Oxford University Press, 1997.

———. "Ways Women Lead." *Harvard Business Review*, November-December 1990.

"The Royal Treatment." www.cbsnews.com/stories/2003/04/18/60minutes.

Sellers, Patricia. "Power: Do Women Really Want It?" *Fortune*, October 13, 2003.

Tannen, Deborah. *You Just Don't Understand: Women and Men in Conversation.* New York: William Morrow, 1990.

Tichy, Noel. *The Leadership Engine.* New York: HarperBusiness, 2002.

Van der Werff, Terry J. "Where Will the Workers Come From?" *Global Future Report*, October 5, 1998.

Women and Diversity. *WOW! Facts 2002.* 3rd ed. Washington, DC: The Business Women's Network, 2002.

Index

African Americans, workplace
  perspectives, 40
alternative work arrangements,
  104–5
ambiguity, as leadership challenge,
  159-60
American Airlines, 15
American Express Company, 126-
  27
America's Competitive Secret:
  Woman Managers (Rosener), 56-
  57
Apgar, Mahlon IV, 104
Asians, workplace perspectives, 40

bad experiences, male and female
  approaches to, 72
Barker, Joel, 24
benchmark companies, 22–23
bench strength, retaining, as
  leadership challenge, 155–57
Bennis, Warren G., 6, 80, 84
Blockbuster, 151-52
The BodyShop, 130

Boone, Garrett, 133-34
BrainStyles®, 62
Burrus, Dan, 93–94
Bush, Linda, 61–62
business relationships, male and
  female approaches to, 71

Carty, Don, 15
CEOs
  buy-in of, required for change,
    23–24
  need to educate, 21–22
  old-style, 51–52, 120
  personal experience of, leading
    to different perspective, 22
change
  as leadership challenge, 148-49
  motivation for, 23–24
Chenault, Ken, 126-27
children, gender roles assigned
  to, 59-61
Claes, Marie-Therese, 58
collaborative cross-functional
  stretchpoint teams, 107, 111,

113–15, 119
collaborative cross-functional
    teams, 113
collaborative teams, 112–13, 120,
    130, 145
Collins, Jim, 10
communication, 130
    listening required for, 82
    male and female approaches to,
    70
    transparent, 90, 94, 134, 144,
    149
compensation programs,
    encouraging individual
    competition, 129
competition, within companies,
    17–19
conflict, 158-59
    male and female approaches to,
    71
The Container Store, 133-34
contingency workers, 35
Covey, Stephen, 147
cross-functional experience, 130
culture change, as leadership
    challenge, 148-49

day care centers, onsite, 36–37
decentralization, 119
decision making
    male and female approaches to,
    72
    self-assessment of, 141
Dell, 118
Demby, Elayne Robertson, 146
depression, 61
Dillman, Linda, 134
disconnected employees, 3–6, 7,
    9, 13–14, 16–17 20, 95
diversity

global, 6
    recruitment and development
    for, 132
    redefining for twenty-first
    century, 42–45, 105-6, 107–8
    resistance to, 28–30
    workforce, 9–10
Dixon, Patrick, 97
do-unto-others business
    philosophy, 140
Drucker, Peter, 95

Eagly, Alice, 57, 69
Edward Jones, 23, 128-30
egos, role in leadership, 25–26
elder care assistance, companies
    offering, 35–36
Eli Lilly, 131- 33
emotional discipline, 90, 92, 141
Emotional Intelligence (Goleman),
    92
emotions
    expressing, in workplace, 61
    male and female approaches to,
    72
empathy, 22
employees
    challenging employers, 48,
    50–51
    commitment to companies,
    48–49
    as company's primary asset, 58,
    74, 95, 97–98, 146
    empowerment of, 118-20
    motivating, 98–99
    optimizing contribution of,
    96–97, 101–2
    optimizing skills of, 47–49
employers of choice,
    characteristics of, 23

empowerment, 118-20
ethical behavior, 86-88
Evans, Warren, 17

Felker, Vicki, 134
Finley, Guy, 10
flexibility, 68, 84, 91-92, 130
flexible work schedules, 23, 36,
    103, 142
focus, key areas of, for men and
    women, 69-74
Ford Motor Company, 36
Fudge, Ann, 130-31

Gandhi, Mahatma, 66
Generation X, workplace
    perspectives, 38
Giuliani, Rudolph, 30-31
glass ceiling, 27, 57
Goleman, Daniel, 92
Goodnight, Jim, 125-26, 145
Google, 78

Hansen, Mike, 134
hard wiring, 59-63
The Heart of Change (Kotter), 154
Helmstetter, Shad, 63
Her Corner Office (Bourgeois),
    103, 140, 166
Herman, Roger, 103
Himsel, Deborrah, 146
Hispanics, workplace
    perspectives, 41
Holmes, Michael, 5, 129-30
humility, 25
humor, 78, 121-22
hybrid leaders
    assessment for, 66
    characteristics of, 56-60, 64-

65, 74-75, 79-83
    communication skills, 94
    competency matrix, 80
    connecting with employees,
        78-79
    encouraging collaboration, 107
    flexibility of, 91-92
    focus on people as
        organization's greatest asset,
        95-96
    key leadership principles, 141-
        43
    obtaining full commitment
        from employees, 101-2
    personal business principles, 86
    principles for leadership, 77
    responsibilities of, 89-90, 96,
        102
    root system of, 79-83
    setting an example, 91, 148
    strategic planning, 92-94
    tips for, 146-60, 163-65
    viewing leadership as service
        role, 100-101

illness, related to attitude toward
    work, 4-5
inclusion, as leadership
    challenge, 157-58
information gathering, male and
    female approaches to, 73
innovation, 107-8
    as leadership challenge, 151-52
internal surveys, 129
interpersonal skills, 144

job sharing, 36

Kimberly-Clark, 35
Kotter, John P., 6, 144, 154

leaders. *See also* hybrid leaders
  demonstrating by example, 133
  desired characteristics, from
    employees' perspective, 55-56
  making changes around, 10-11
  self-assessment for, 126-27
  valuing people, 143-45
leadership. *See also* leadership
  challenges
  characteristics desired for, 64-
    65
  command-and-control, 25-26
  double standard for men and
    women, 63-64
  at every organizational level,
    102
  images of, 63-64
  military style, 6
  need for accountability among,
    24-25
  primary contributor to
    workplace problems, 5
  shared, 121
  style differences for men and
    women, 67-69, 74
  top-down, 6
Leadership (Giuliani), 30-31
leadership challenges
  ambiguity, 159-60
  change, 148-49
  conflict, 158-59
  culture change, 148-49
  inclusion, 157-58
  innovation for future success,
    107-8
  perceptions of black women,
    149-50
  personal growth, 152-53

retaining bench strength, 155-57
team performance improve-
  ment, 14-487
women at the top, 160-61
Leading Change (Kotter), 144
learning, continuous
  commitment to, 99-100
Leff, Dessie, 146
Legato, Marianne, 69
loyalty, perception of leadership
  related to, 16

men
  commitment to parenting
    responsibilities, 83
  key areas of focus for, 69-73
  leadership style for, 67-69, 83
  stereotypes about, 64-65
minorities, workplace
  perspectives, 41
mission statements, 30, 115-16,
  127
Morgane, Maurice, 134
motivation, 76, 78, 85, 98-99

negotiations, male and female
  approaches to, 70
Nestlé Purina Pet Care, 99-100
nontraditional needs, 103-5

older employees, workplace
  perspectives, 39
organizational culture, 9

perceptions of black women, as
  leadership challenge, 149-50
personal agendas, negative impact
  of, 19-20
personal development matrix,
  140

personal growth, as leadership challenge, 152-53
personal transformation model, 175-76
Peterson, P. Michael, 4–5
Pogue, Richard, 134
Potter, Ed, 45
Pour Your Heart into It: How Starbucks Built a Company One Cup at a Time (Schultz), 127-28
power, male and female approaches to, 71-72
problem solving, male and female approaches to, 72
The Purpose-Driven Life (Warren), 46

real-time learning, 116–18
relationship management, 47
results, focus on, 143
retention strategy, 27, 129
retirement, replacing workers, 45
risk taking, 49–51
Roddick, Anita, 130–31
Romig, Denis A., 120
Rosener, Judy, 56

SAS, 145
Scelz, Rebecca, 134
Schmit, Eric, 78
Schultz, Howard, 128
Sears Corporation, 109, 117–18
self-assessment, for leaders, 126-27
self-discovery, 84–85
self-talk, 63
September 11, 2001, 15, 122, 126
7-Eleven, 118
shared leadership, 121

Side by Side Leadership (Romig), 120
silos, 17–19, 106–7
skilled-labor shortage, 14, 27, 30, 48, 103
small companies, women moving to, 27–28
Smith, Rick, 131-133
Southwest Airlines, 122
spiritual rituals, companies respecting, 36
Starbucks, 127-28, 130
Steele, Marcia, 93
stereotypes, overcoming, 62, 64, 121
strategic planning, 92–94
stress-related absence, 5
stress relief, male and female approaches to, 73
stretchpoint teams, 114-17
succession plan, 155-56

talent, getting and keeping, 103–5
Tannen, Deborah, 59
Taurel, Sidney, 132
Teague, Juanell, 99
team performance improvement, as leadership challenge, 147-48
teams. *See also* collaborative cross-functional stretchpoint teams, collaborative cross-functional teams, collaborative teams. characteristics needed for breakthrough performance, 120-21
telecommuting, 36
thinking process, male and female approaches to, 69

Tichy, Noel, 107-8, 136
time zero, 62
Tindell, Kip, 134
Trust
  employees' loss of, in
    organizations, 9
  lack of, impact on business
    results, 19-20
Trust and Effectiveness Survey, 9
turnover, 14

unethical corporate behavior,
  response to, 17

Van der Werff, Terry J., 103
vision statements, 30, 116, 126

Wal-Mart, 76, 117-18, 165
Warren, Rick, 46
water cooler discussions, 78
white males, workplace
  perspectives, 40
White, James, 99
Whetmore, Don, 4
Whole Foods, 119
women
  increased role for, as leaders,
  27-28

key areas of focus for, 69-73
leadership style for, 67-69,
  83-84
stereotypes about, 64-65
at the top, as leadership
  challenge, 160-61
value of, in workplace, 56-57
workplace perspectives, 38-39
workforce
  changes in, over last quarter-
    century, 33-35
  demographics of, in twenty-first
    century, 35, 44-45
Workforce 2020, 6
work/life balance, 37-38, 45-47,
  98, 102-4
workplace
  companies slow to change in,
    21-22
  fun and humor in, 121-22
  I vs. we mentality in, 7-9
  perspectives on, of different
    groups, 38-42
  showing emotion in, 61, 72-73
  theft of ideas in, 7-9
  values of, male and female
    approaches to, 73

Young & Rubicam Brands, 130

Recommended Reading

In addition to the books, articles and whitepapers listed in the bibliography which I highly recommend that you read, I also suggest that you consider reading the following books. I have found these books to be informative and helpful.

The Dalai Lama and Howard C. Cutler, M.D. *The Art of Happiness at Work*, Riverhead Books (A member of Penguin Group) New York 2003

Lynne C. Lancaster and David Stillman, *When Generations Collide*, Collins Business 2002

Leigh Branham, *The 7 Hidden Reasons Employees Leave*, American Management Association, New York 2005

Daniel H. Pink, *A Whole New Mind: Moving from the Information Age to the Conceptual Age*, Riverhead Books, New York 2005

Hunter Lawrence, The Servant: *A Simple Story About the True Essence of Leadership*, Crown Business 1998

Ken Blanchard and Phil Hodges, *The Servant Leader: Transforming Your Heart, Head, Hands & Habits*, Countryman, Nashville, Tennessee 2003

Marlane Miller, *Brainstyles: Change Your Life Without Changing Who You Are*, Simon and Schuster 1997

James O. Rodgers with Maureen Hunter, Ph.D., *Managing Differently: Getting 100% from 100% of Your People 100% of the Time*, Oakhill Press 2004

Developmental Resources for Success

by Trudy Bourgeois

Books:

Her Corner Office: A Guide to Help Women Find a Place and a Voice in Corporate America

Price: $19.95 (Available in book stores everyone, or order on line www.workforceexcellence.com)

This book is loaded with practical strategies, tips and insights to help women enhance their leadership effectiveness and career advancement.

Key areas covered include

- Why success starts with taking personal responsibility
- The key elements of a successful career advancement strategy
- The five critical components for women to establish themselves as leaders
- How to overcome stereotypes that limit advancement

- Savvy personal marketing strategies
- How to leverage the natural feminine traits
- Insights on communicating with power and conviction
- Why women will play a critical role in reshaping corporate America

Audio CD's

(Available only by ordering on-line www.workforceexcellence.com)

10 PRINCIPLES TO DEVELOP YOUR LEADERSHIP SKILLS

What will it take to mobilize the organization to achieve breakthrough performance? The answer is great leaders. This program will provide you with ten key principles that will enhance your leadership capabilities to show you how to connect you with your team, and coach them to success.

Price: $15.00

THE HYBRID LEADER

Successful leaders in the 21st Century are collaborative, open, focused on serving others, harnessing the greatness of others and truly dedicated to breakthrough results. This combination of skills will only come from blending the best of the male and female leadership behaviors, values and traits.

Price: $15.00

THE OPPORTUNITY CALLED CHANGE

To experience profound success in the 21st Century everyone must learn how to embrace change as an opportunity. Your abilities can only be optimized through continuous learning, exploration, flexibility and a willingness to step boldly into the unknown.

Price: $15.00

ON YOUR WAY TO THE TOP

Have you ever wondered why some people experience career success, getting one promotion after another, while others stay in the same position year after year? Maybe they are lucky, or maybe they know the value of their personal brand and have designed a personal marketing plan to increase their visibility and credibility. In this powerful program, you will get the inside secrets needed to develop and implement a tangible, proven personal marketing strategy.

Price: $15.00

DREAM BIG, AIM FOR THE STARS

Life is full of opportunities, challenges, setbacks and disappointments. The one constant amidst all of these elements is the power of personal choice. When you have clarity of a personal vision and take personal responsibility for yourself you can find the courage to make the choices that will guarantee you the greatest chances of success in life.

Price: $15.00

Special Packages:

On Your Way to the Top: Marketing Your Way to Success

CD and Manual
Price: $49.95

Was Trudy's book helpful to you? Here are some Oakhill Press titles you'll want to read:

PEOPLE-SMART LEADERS
Maximizing people performance and profits

1-886939-61-6

Larry Cole, $22.95

Details how to maximize people performance and profits by improving the interpersonal behaviors of your individual team members.

DISTINGUISHING MARKS OF A LEADER:
How you can think, act, and earn like a leading salesperson

1-886939-65-9

Mark Leader, $24.95

Gathers traits and characteristics of outstanding performers in the sales industry so that you can emulate them and become a leader.

I DIDN'T ASK YOU TO DANCE, I ASKED YOU TO TALK!
A common sense, humorous, and at times spiritual approach to communication in a world obsessed with political correctness

1-886939-62-4

Maxie Carpenter, $19.95

Offers a collection of practical, real-life experiences everyone can relate to, from business managers to board members, church-leaders to humorists.

HAVE A GREAT YEAR EVERY YEAR
A Four-Point Program for Maximizing Your Performance

1-886939-69-1

Dave Yoho, $21.95

Galvanizes human resources with a simple four-point program tackling the aspects of business life that can make or break a company.

KEEPING GOOD PEOPLE

Strategies for Solving the #1 Problem Facing Businesses Today

1-886939-26-8

Roger Herman, $21.95

Explains, in conversational and practical language, everything employers need to know for great employee retention.

Purchase at your local bookstore, Amazon.com, BN.com
and other online booksellers, or contact:

Oakhill Press

1647 Cedar Grove Road

Winchester, VA 22603

800-32-BOOKS (800-322-6657)

www.oakhillpress.com